Essential Accounting Practices

Effective Strategies for Accurate Financial Reporting
and Business Decision-Making

Jonathan A. Clark

Essential Accounting Practices

TABLE OF CONTENTS

Chapter 1: Introduction to Essential Accounting Practices

The Role of Accounting in Business

Accounting plays an indispensable role in the business world, serving as the backbone of financial management and decision-making. At its core, accounting involves the systematic recording, analyzing, and reporting of financial transactions. This process allows businesses to maintain accurate records of their operations, ensuring transparency and accountability. By providing a clear picture of a company's financial health, accounting helps stakeholders make informed decisions, fostering trust and confidence in the business's sustainability and growth potential.

The role of accounting extends far beyond mere number-crunching. It is integral to every aspect of business, from day-to-day operations to strategic planning. Accurate accounting practices enable businesses to track income and expenses meticulously, ensuring that financial statements reflect the true state of affairs. This accuracy is crucial for assessing profitability, managing cash flow, and identifying areas where cost-cutting measures might be necessary. Moreover, reliable financial data is essential for complying with regulatory requirements and avoiding legal complications.

One of the primary functions of accounting in business is to facilitate financial reporting. Financial reports, such as balance sheets, income statements, and cash flow statements, provide a snapshot of the company's performance over a specific period.

These reports are vital tools for internal management and external stakeholders, including investors, creditors, and regulatory bodies. For instance, a balance sheet offers a detailed view of the company's assets, liabilities, and equity at a given point in time, helping stakeholders assess its financial stability. An income statement, on the other hand, outlines revenues and expenses, highlighting the company's profitability. The cash flow statement tracks the flow of cash in and out of the business, providing insights into its liquidity and operational efficiency.

Beyond financial reporting, accounting plays a crucial role in strategic decision-making. By analyzing financial data, businesses can identify trends, forecast future performance, and make informed decisions about investments, expansions, and cost management. For example, through variance analysis, managers can compare actual financial performance against budgeted figures, pinpointing discrepancies and taking corrective actions. This proactive approach helps businesses stay on track with their financial goals and adapt to changing market conditions.

In addition to influencing strategic decisions, accounting is essential for budgeting and financial planning. Budgets serve as financial blueprints, guiding businesses in allocating resources efficiently and setting financial targets. Accounting provides the data needed to create realistic budgets and monitor performance against these plans. Effective budgeting ensures that businesses do not overspend and helps them prioritize investments that offer the best returns. Furthermore, accurate financial planning enables businesses to prepare for future financial needs, such as funding expansions, managing debt, and weathering economic downturns.

Accounting also plays a pivotal role in risk management and internal controls. By maintaining detailed financial records, businesses can detect and prevent fraudulent activities, ensuring the integrity of their financial data. Internal controls, such as segregation of duties and regular audits, help safeguard assets and ensure that financial transactions are conducted in accordance with established policies. These measures not only protect the company from financial loss but also enhance its reputation by demonstrating a commitment to ethical practices and regulatory compliance.

The role of accounting in business extends to tax compliance as well. Accurate accounting records are essential for calculating tax liabilities and ensuring timely payment of taxes. Businesses must adhere to various tax regulations, and failure to comply can result in penalties and damage to their reputation. Accounting helps businesses navigate the complexities of tax laws, optimize their tax positions, and avoid legal issues. By keeping meticulous records, businesses can also take advantage of tax deductions and credits, reducing their overall tax burden.

Another critical aspect of accounting is its contribution to stakeholder communication. Transparent and accurate financial reporting fosters trust among investors, creditors, employees, and other stakeholders. Investors rely on financial statements to assess the viability and profitability of their investments. Creditors use these reports to evaluate the company's creditworthiness and decide whether to extend credit. Employees, too, benefit from understanding the company's financial health, as it impacts job security and performance-based incentives. Clear and honest communication through financial reporting helps build strong relationships with stakeholders, ensuring their continued support and engagement.

Accounting's role in business is also evident in performance measurement and management. By setting financial benchmarks and key performance indicators (KPIs), businesses can measure their progress toward achieving strategic objectives. Accounting provides the data needed to track these KPIs, enabling managers to evaluate performance and make data-driven decisions. For instance, profitability ratios, liquidity ratios, and efficiency ratios offer insights into various aspects of the company's operations, helping managers identify strengths and weaknesses. Regular performance reviews based on accounting data ensure that businesses stay aligned with their goals and make necessary adjustments to improve performance.

Moreover, accounting facilitates operational efficiency by streamlining financial processes and systems. The implementation of accounting software and technologies automates routine tasks, reducing the likelihood of errors and freeing up resources for more strategic activities. For example, automated invoicing and payment systems enhance cash flow management, while integrated financial reporting tools provide real-time insights into financial performance. By leveraging technology, businesses can enhance their accounting practices, ensuring accuracy, efficiency, and compliance.

In conclusion, accounting is a fundamental component of business operations, underpinning financial management, strategic planning, and decision-making.

Accurate financial reporting is the bedrock upon which sound business decisions are made. It involves the precise and truthful representation of a company's financial transactions and condition. This transparency is vital not only for internal stakeholders, such as management and employees, but also for external parties including investors, creditors, and regulatory bodies. Accurate financial reporting ensures that all these parties have a clear and honest view of the company's financial health, which is crucial for fostering trust and facilitating informed decision-making.

One of the primary reasons accurate financial reporting is essential lies in its role in decision-making processes. Managers rely on financial reports to make strategic decisions about the direction of the company. For instance, a detailed income statement can reveal which products or services are most profitable, guiding decisions about where to invest resources. Similarly, a well-prepared balance sheet offers insights into the company's liquidity and financial stability, which are crucial for planning future investments or expansions. Without accurate data, these decisions would be based on guesswork, increasing the risk of poor outcomes.

Investors are another group that heavily relies on accurate financial reporting. When investors consider putting money into a company, they scrutinize its financial statements to assess the potential return on their investment. They look at indicators such as revenue growth, profit margins, and debt levels to gauge the company's performance and prospects. If the financial reports are inaccurate, investors may be misled into making poor investment choices. This not only harms the investors but can also damage the company's reputation and ability to raise capital in the future.

Creditors, including banks and other lending institutions, also depend on accurate financial reporting to evaluate a company's creditworthiness. Accurate financial statements help creditors determine whether a business can meet its debt obligations. For instance, they look at cash flow statements to ensure the company generates enough cash to cover loan repayments. If the reports are inaccurate, creditors might either extend credit to a company that is a high risk or deny credit to a business that is actually financially sound. Both scenarios can have significant negative consequences for the business.

Regulatory compliance is another critical aspect of accurate financial reporting. Companies are required by law to maintain truthful and precise financial records. Regulatory bodies, such as the Securities and Exchange Commission (SEC) in the United States, enforce these requirements to protect investors and maintain market integrity. Inaccurate financial reporting can lead to severe penalties, including fines and legal action. Moreover, it can result in a loss of confidence among investors and the public, which can be difficult to restore.

In addition to these external factors, accurate financial reporting is crucial for internal controls and fraud prevention. By maintaining detailed and correct records, companies can implement effective internal controls to monitor and manage financial activities. Accurate reporting makes it easier to detect discrepancies and unusual transactions that could indicate fraud or embezzlement. This not only protects the company's assets but also ensures that financial statements truly reflect the company's performance.

Accurate financial reporting is also vital for tax purposes. Businesses must provide precise financial information to tax authorities to calculate their tax liabilities correctly. Underreporting income or overstating expenses can lead to tax evasion charges, while overreporting can result in paying more taxes than necessary. Both scenarios can have significant financial repercussions. Accurate reporting ensures that companies comply with tax laws and optimize their tax positions, taking advantage of all available deductions and credits.

The significance of accurate financial reporting extends to performance measurement and management. Companies set financial targets and measure their performance against these goals using key performance indicators (KPIs). Accurate financial data is essential for tracking these KPIs and evaluating whether the company is meeting its strategic objectives. For instance, profitability ratios, efficiency ratios, and liquidity ratios are all derived from financial reports. If these reports are inaccurate, the resulting ratios and performance measures will be misleading, potentially leading to incorrect conclusions and poor management decisions.

Accurate financial reporting also plays a crucial role in maintaining stakeholder trust. Employees, customers, suppliers, and the community at large all have a vested interest in the company's success and sustainability. Transparent and accurate financial reporting demonstrates the company's commitment to honesty and ethical practices. This fosters a positive reputation and strengthens relationships with all stakeholders. For example, employees are more likely to remain loyal and motivated if they trust that the company is financially stable and manages its resources responsibly.

Furthermore, accurate financial reporting is essential for business continuity and planning. Companies need precise financial data to develop realistic budgets and forecasts. These financial plans are crucial for setting goals, allocating resources, and preparing for future challenges. Inaccurate reporting can lead to unrealistic budgets and forecasts, resulting in poor financial planning and resource allocation. This can jeopardize the company's ability to achieve its objectives and respond effectively to market changes or economic downturns.

In the era of globalization, accurate financial reporting is even more critical as companies operate across multiple jurisdictions with varying accounting standards. Ensuring that financial reports are accurate and comply with international standards, such as the International Financial Reporting Standards (IFRS), is essential for multinational companies. This not only facilitates cross-border operations and investments but also ensures that the company meets the regulatory requirements of all the countries in which it operates.

Technology also plays a significant role in enhancing the accuracy of financial reporting. The advent of advanced accounting software and automated systems has revolutionized how financial data is recorded, processed, and reported. These tools reduce human error and increase efficiency, ensuring that financial reports are both timely and accurate. For instance, automated reconciliation tools can quickly identify and resolve discrepancies in financial records, while integrated systems can ensure that all transactions are consistently recorded across different departments and locations. By leveraging technology, businesses can maintain high standards of accuracy in their financial reporting, which is critical for making informed decisions and maintaining stakeholder trust.

Effective strategic decision-making in business hinges on the adept use of financial data. This chapter delves into the integration of financial information into the strategic planning process, providing a guide for leveraging these insights to drive informed decisions that propel a business towards its goals.

Understanding the role of financial data begins with recognizing its multifaceted nature. Financial data encompasses a range of information, from revenue and expenses to cash flows and balance sheet items. Each piece of data contributes to a comprehensive picture of a company's financial health and operational efficiency. For strategic decision-making, it is crucial to distill this data into actionable insights.

One of the primary tools for this purpose is financial ratio analysis. Ratios such as the current ratio, quick ratio, debt-to-equity ratio, and return on equity offer snapshots of various aspects of financial performance. For instance, the current ratio, which compares current assets to current liabilities, indicates the company's ability to meet short-term obligations. A high current ratio suggests sound liquidity, which can influence decisions related to investments, expansions, or debt repayments. Similarly, the debt-to-equity ratio provides insight into the company's financial leverage and risk profile, guiding strategic choices about capital structure and funding sources.

Beyond ratios, trend analysis offers another layer of insight. By examining financial data over multiple periods, businesses can identify patterns and trends that inform strategic decisions. For example, a consistent increase in operating expenses might signal the need for cost control measures or a review of operational efficiencies. Conversely, a steady rise in revenue might justify expansion plans or increased investment in marketing initiatives.

Scenario analysis and forecasting are also integral to strategic decision-making. These techniques involve projecting future financial performance under various hypothetical scenarios. By adjusting variables such as sales growth rates, cost structures, and market conditions, businesses can evaluate potential outcomes and develop strategies that align with their goals. For instance, a company might use scenario analysis to assess the impact of entering a new market, considering best-case, worst-case, and most-likely scenarios to guide their decision.

Cash flow analysis is another critical component of strategic decision-making. Understanding cash inflows and outflows helps businesses manage liquidity and ensure they have the necessary funds to support their strategic initiatives. Cash flow projections can inform decisions about capital expenditures, debt financing, and working capital management. For instance, a positive cash flow forecast might support a decision to invest in new equipment, while a negative forecast might prompt measures to improve cash collections or reduce expenses.

Benchmarking against industry standards provides additional context for financial data. By comparing their performance to peers and industry averages, businesses can identify strengths and weaknesses in their financial position. This comparative analysis can highlight areas for improvement and guide strategic priorities. For example, if a company's profit margin is below the industry average, it might explore ways to increase efficiency or adjust pricing strategies.

Integration of financial data into strategic planning requires a systematic approach. First, businesses must ensure the accuracy and reliability of their financial data. This involves maintaining robust accounting systems and internal controls, regularly reconciling accounts, and conducting audits. Accurate data is the foundation upon which sound strategic decisions are built.

Next, the data must be analyzed and interpreted in the context of the business's strategic objectives. This involves collaboration between financial analysts, accountants, and strategic planners. By working together, these professionals can translate financial data into strategic insights. For instance, financial analysts might identify trends in revenue growth, while strategic planners assess how these trends align with the company's long-term goals.

Effective communication of financial insights is also crucial. Decision-makers must have a clear understanding of the financial implications of their choices. This requires presenting financial data in a user-friendly format, using visual aids such as charts and graphs to illustrate key points. Clear and concise communication ensures that stakeholders can grasp the significance of the data and make informed decisions.

Incorporating financial data into strategic decision-making also involves considering external factors. Market conditions, economic trends, and regulatory changes can all impact financial performance and strategic choices. For example, a downturn in the economy might prompt a business to adopt a more conservative approach, focusing on cost control and liquidity management. Conversely, a favorable market environment might encourage more aggressive growth strategies.

Risk management is another critical aspect of strategic decision-making with financial data. Businesses must assess the financial risks associated with their strategic choices and develop plans to mitigate these risks. This involves identifying potential financial pitfalls, such as fluctuations in revenue, increases in costs, or changes in interest rates. By proactively managing these risks, businesses can protect their financial stability and support long-term success.

Technology also plays a significant role in leveraging financial data for strategic decision-making. Advanced financial software and analytics tools enable businesses to process large volumes of data quickly and accurately. These tools can automate routine tasks, generate detailed reports, and provide real-time insights, enhancing the decision-making process. For example, predictive analytics can forecast future financial performance based on historical data, helping businesses plan more effectively.

Furthermore, businesses must foster a culture that values data-driven decision-making. This involves training employees at all levels to understand and use financial data in their roles. By promoting financial literacy across the organization, companies can ensure that everyone is aligned with the strategic objectives and able to contribute to informed decision-making. This culture of data-driven decision-making extends beyond the finance department to include managers and employees in all areas of the business.

Accounting serves as the backbone of any business, providing the essential information needed to make informed decisions. Understanding key accounting concepts is crucial for anyone involved in managing or running a business. These concepts form the foundation of accounting practices and ensure that financial information is recorded, classified, and interpreted accurately.

At the heart of accounting lies the accounting equation: Assets = Liabilities + Equity. This fundamental equation represents the relationship between what a business owns and what it owes, along with the owner's interest in the company. Every financial transaction impacts this equation, maintaining its balance. For example, when a company takes out a loan, it increases both its assets (cash) and its liabilities (loan payable), keeping the equation in balance.

The dual aspect of every transaction is captured through double-entry bookkeeping, a system where each transaction affects at least two accounts. This method ensures accuracy and completeness in financial records. For instance, purchasing inventory with cash decreases the cash account and increases the inventory account. This system helps in detecting errors and maintaining the integrity of financial data.

Accrual accounting, as opposed to cash accounting, recognizes revenues and expenses when they are earned or incurred, regardless of when the cash is actually received or paid. This approach provides a more accurate picture of a company's financial position and performance. For example, if a company delivers a service in December but receives payment in January, the revenue is recorded in December under accrual accounting. This principle aligns with the matching concept, which dictates that expenses should be matched with the revenues they help generate within the same period. This ensures that financial statements reflect the true costs associated with generating revenue.

Revenue recognition is another key concept. The revenue recognition principle states that revenue should be recognized when it is earned and realizable, not necessarily when cash is received. This principle helps in presenting a more accurate and consistent view of a company's financial performance. For example, a company that sells goods on credit will recognize the revenue at the point of sale, even though the cash will be received later.

The historical cost principle dictates that assets should be recorded at their original purchase price. This provides consistency and reliability in financial reporting, as historical costs are verifiable and objective. For instance, if a company buys a piece of equipment for $10,000, it will record the equipment at this cost, regardless of its market value in subsequent periods.

Depreciation and amortization are methods used to allocate the cost of tangible and intangible assets over their useful lives. Depreciation applies to physical assets like machinery and buildings, while amortization applies to intangible assets like patents and trademarks. These processes ensure that the expense of using an asset is recognized over the period it benefits the company. For example, if a company purchases a machine for $50,000 with a useful life of 10 years, it might depreciate the machine at $5,000 per year.

The concept of consistency requires that a company applies the same accounting principles and methods from period to period. This enhances comparability of financial statements over time. Any changes in accounting policies must be disclosed and justified. For example, if a company switches from straight-line depreciation to an accelerated method, it must disclose this change and its impact on the financial statements.

Materiality is another important concept, referring to the significance of financial information. An item is considered material if its omission or misstatement could influence the economic decisions of users. This concept helps accountants decide what information should be included in financial statements. For example, a $500 error in a large corporation's financial statements might be immaterial, but the same error could be significant for a small business.

The principle of conservatism guides accountants to choose solutions that result in lower profits and asset valuations when faced with uncertainty. This means recognizing expenses and liabilities as soon as possible, but only recognizing revenues and assets when they are assured. For instance, if there is doubt about the collectability of a receivable, a conservative approach would be to record an allowance for doubtful accounts.

Another key concept is the going concern assumption, which assumes that a business will continue to operate indefinitely, unless there is evidence to the contrary. This assumption underlies the preparation of financial statements, as it affects the valuation of assets and liabilities. If a company is not considered a going concern, it might need to liquidate its assets at less than their book value.

The economic entity concept states that a business must be treated as a separate entity from its owners and any other business entities. This ensures that the financial activities of the business are recorded and reported independently of the personal financial activities of its owners. For example, the expenses incurred by the owner for personal travel should not be recorded as business expenses.

The time period concept, also known as the periodicity assumption, allows companies to report financial results over regular intervals, such as months, quarters, or years. This enables stakeholders to assess the company's performance and make timely decisions. For instance, publicly traded companies are required to file quarterly and annual financial statements.

Lastly, the full disclosure principle requires that all relevant financial information be disclosed in the financial statements or accompanying notes. This ensures that users of financial statements have all the information necessary to make informed decisions. This includes details about accounting policies, potential liabilities, and any other significant events that could impact the financial position of the company. For instance, if a company is facing a significant lawsuit, it must disclose this fact along with any potential financial implications.

Chapter 2: The Accounting Cycle and Financial Statements

Understanding the Accounting Cycle

The accounting cycle is the backbone of any robust financial management system. It comprises a series of steps that companies follow to identify, analyze, and record their financial transactions. Understanding this cycle is fundamental for anyone involved in the financial aspects of a business, from beginners to seasoned professionals. By mastering the accounting cycle, one ensures that financial data is accurate, complete, and in compliance with accounting standards, which is essential for sound decision-making and financial reporting.

The accounting cycle begins with the identification and analysis of transactions. Every business transaction must be documented with evidence such as invoices, receipts, and bank statements. This initial step is crucial because it provides the raw data needed for the subsequent stages of the cycle. For instance, when a company makes a sale, the transaction is recorded with an invoice that details the amount, date, and items sold. Similarly, expenses are documented with receipts and bills that specify the cost, date, and nature of the expenditure. Proper documentation ensures that all transactions are captured accurately and can be referenced or audited later.

Once transactions are identified and analyzed, they must be recorded in the journal. The journal, often referred to as the book of original entry, is where transactions are logged in chronological order. Each entry in the journal includes the date of the transaction, the accounts affected, and the amounts debited and credited. This process, known as journalizing, is critical because it lays the foundation for all subsequent financial reporting. For example, if a business purchases office supplies on credit, the journal entry would debit the office supplies account and credit the accounts payable account. This dual-entry system ensures that the accounting equation (Assets = Liabilities + Equity) remains balanced.

After journalizing transactions, the next step is posting them to the ledger. The ledger is a collection of accounts that shows the changes made to each account as a result of the transactions recorded in the journal. Each account in the ledger has its own page or section where all debits and credits related to that account are posted. For instance, all transactions affecting the cash account are posted to the cash ledger, providing a comprehensive view of cash inflows and outflows over a specific period. This step helps in organizing and summarizing financial data, making it easier to prepare financial statements.

Once transactions are posted to the ledger, the trial balance is prepared. The trial balance is a list of all ledger accounts and their balances at a specific point in time. It is used to verify that the total debits equal the total credits, ensuring the accuracy of the books. If the trial balance does not balance, it indicates that there are errors in the journalizing or posting processes that need to be identified and corrected. For example, if a transaction was recorded with a debit to the cash account but no corresponding credit, the trial balance would reveal a discrepancy that must be investigated and resolved.

Adjusting entries are the next critical step in the accounting cycle. These entries are made at the end of an accounting period to ensure that revenues and expenses are recognized in the period in which they occur, in accordance with the matching principle. Common adjusting entries include accruals, deferrals, and estimates. For instance, if a business incurs interest on a loan but hasn't yet paid it by the end of the period, an adjusting entry is made to accrue the interest expense. Similarly, if rent is paid in advance, a deferral entry is made to record the rent expense over the periods it benefits. Adjusting entries are essential for ensuring that financial statements reflect the true financial position and performance of the business.

Once adjusting entries are made, an adjusted trial balance is prepared. This is similar to the initial trial balance but includes the effects of the adjusting entries. The adjusted trial balance is used to prepare the financial statements, ensuring that all accounts are up to date and accurate. The accuracy of the adjusted trial balance is crucial because it directly impacts the financial statements, which are used by stakeholders to make informed decisions.

The preparation of financial statements follows the adjusted trial balance. The primary financial statements include the income statement, balance sheet, and statement of cash flows. The income statement shows the company's revenues and expenses over a specific period, resulting in net income or loss. The balance sheet provides a snapshot of the company's assets, liabilities, and equity at a specific point in time. The statement of cash flows details the cash inflows and outflows from operating, investing, and financing activities. These statements provide a comprehensive view of the company's financial health, performance, and cash management.

After the financial statements are prepared, closing entries are made to reset the balances of temporary accounts (revenues, expenses, and dividends) to zero for the next accounting period. This step involves transferring the balances of these accounts to the retained earnings account. For example, if a company had $100,000 in revenue and $60,000 in expenses for the period, the closing entries would transfer the net income of $40,000 to retained earnings. This ensures that only the balances of permanent accounts (assets, liabilities, and equity) are carried forward to the next period , maintaining a clean slate for the new accounting period. Closing entries are essential for accurate financial reporting and analysis, as they ensure that income and expense accounts reflect activity solely from the current period, preventing any carryover that could distort future financial statements.

Recording transactions is a fundamental aspect of accounting that ensures financial data is accurately captured and maintained. The process involves two critical components: journals and ledgers. These tools provide a systematic way to document and organize financial transactions, forming the basis for preparing financial statements and making informed business decisions.

Imagine a small bakery, Sweet Treats, which has just opened its doors. The owner, Emma, needs to keep track of every financial transaction, from purchasing ingredients to selling pastries. Emma's journey into the world of accounting begins with recording transactions in the journal, also known as the book of original entry. This is where all financial transactions are first recorded in chronological order. Each entry in the journal includes the date, accounts affected, and amounts debited and credited, accompanied by a brief description of the transaction.

For instance, on the opening day, Emma purchases flour, sugar, and other baking supplies for $500 on credit. The journal entry for this transaction would debit the Supplies account and credit Accounts Payable, reflecting an increase in supplies and a corresponding liability. By recording this transaction, Emma ensures that the purchase is documented and can be traced back for future reference or audits.

As transactions accumulate, the next step is to post them to the ledger, which is a collection of accounts that summarizes all transactions affecting each account. The ledger provides a more organized view of financial data, with each account having its own page or section. For Sweet Treats, the ledger would include accounts like Cash, Supplies, Accounts Payable, and Sales. When Emma posts the purchase of supplies to the ledger, she updates the Supplies account with a debit entry and the Accounts Payable account with a credit entry, reflecting the impact of the transaction on each account.

The process of posting to the ledger is crucial because it allows Emma to see the cumulative effect of all transactions on each account. For example, by reviewing the Cash ledger, she can track all cash inflows and outflows, helping her manage the bakery's liquidity. Similarly, the Sales ledger provides a detailed view of all sales transactions, enabling Emma to monitor revenue trends and make strategic decisions about pricing and inventory.

To illustrate the importance of accurate record-keeping, consider a scenario where Emma receives a payment of $200 from a customer for a large order of pastries. She records this transaction in the journal by debiting the Cash account and crediting the Sales account. When she posts this entry to the ledger, she updates the Cash and Sales accounts accordingly. Accurate recording and posting ensure that the bakery's financial statements, such as the income statement and balance sheet, reflect the true financial position and performance of the business.

However, manual recording and posting can be time-consuming and prone to errors. To streamline the process, Emma decides to use accounting software, which automates many aspects of transaction recording. The software allows her to enter transactions once, and it automatically updates the relevant accounts in the ledger. This not only saves time but also reduces the risk of errors, ensuring that the bakery's financial records are accurate and up to date.

In addition to the general journal, Emma may also use special journals for recurring transactions. Special journals, such as the sales journal, purchases journal, cash receipts journal, and cash disbursements journal, help organize similar types of transactions. For example, all sales transactions are recorded in the sales journal, while all cash payments are recorded in the cash disbursements journal. Using special journals can simplify the recording process and make it easier to locate specific transactions.

Once transactions are recorded in the journals and posted to the ledger, Emma prepares a trial balance to verify that total debits equal total credits. This step is essential for ensuring the accuracy of the books. If the trial balance does not balance, it indicates that there may be errors in recording or posting that need to be corrected. For instance, if Emma accidentally recorded a $100 payment as a debit to Cash instead of a credit, the trial balance would reveal this discrepancy, prompting her to identify and fix the mistake.

Accurate recording of transactions also plays a crucial role in financial analysis and decision-making. By maintaining detailed records, Emma can generate financial reports that provide insights into the bakery's performance. For example, by analyzing the Sales ledger, she can identify the most popular products and peak sales periods, helping her optimize inventory and marketing strategies. Similarly, the Expenses ledger allows her to track costs and identify areas where she can reduce expenses and improve profitability.

Moreover, proper transaction recording ensures compliance with accounting standards and regulatory requirements. For instance, if Sweet Treats is audited, having well-organized journals and ledgers makes it easier to provide evidence of financial transactions and demonstrate the accuracy of financial statements. This not only builds trust with stakeholders but also protects the bakery from potential legal and financial issues.

Emma's experience with transaction recording also highlights the importance of internal controls. Internal controls, such as regular reconciliations and segregation of duties, help ensure the accuracy and integrity of financial records. For example, by regularly reconciling the Cash ledger with bank statements, Emma can identify and resolve discrepancies early, preventing potential issues that could arise from unnoticed errors or fraudulent activities. Segregation of duties, where different individuals are responsible for recording transactions, approving payments, and reconciling accounts, adds an additional layer of protection, reducing the risk of fraud and errors.

Preparing Financial Statements: Balance Sheet, Income

Preparing financial statements is a crucial task for any business, as these documents provide a comprehensive overview of the company's financial health and performance. Among these statements, the balance sheet and the income statement are fundamental. They offer insights into a company's financial position at a given point in time and its financial performance over a period, respectively. Understanding how to prepare these statements is essential for business owners, managers, and accountants alike.

The balance sheet, also known as the statement of financial position, provides a snapshot of a company's assets, liabilities, and equity at a specific date. This statement adheres to the accounting equation: Assets = Liabilities + Equity. Preparing a balance sheet involves classifying and valuing the company's resources and obligations.

Assets are divided into current and non-current categories. Current assets include cash and other assets that are expected to be converted into cash or used up within one year, such as accounts receivable, inventory, and prepaid expenses. Non-current assets, also known as long-term assets, include property, plant, and equipment (PP&E), intangible assets like patents and trademarks, and long-term investments. For example, a manufacturing company might list its machinery and factory buildings under non-current assets.

Liabilities are similarly categorized into current and non-current. Current liabilities are obligations the company needs to settle within a year, such as accounts payable, short-term loans, and accrued expenses. Non-current liabilities, or long-term liabilities, are obligations due beyond one year, like long-term debt and deferred tax liabilities. For instance, a company might have a mortgage on its building listed as a non-current liability.

Equity represents the owners' residual interest in the company after liabilities are subtracted from assets. It includes items like common stock, retained earnings, and additional paid-in capital. Retained earnings, in particular, are the cumulative net income that has been reinvested in the business rather than distributed to shareholders as dividends. For example, a company that has been profitable over several years might have substantial retained earnings.

To prepare the balance sheet, one must gather all relevant financial data and ensure it is accurate and up-to-date. This involves reconciling bank statements, verifying receivables and payables, and ensuring that all transactions have been recorded appropriately. Once all data is collected and verified, assets, liabilities, and equity are listed in their respective categories, and the totals are calculated to ensure that the accounting equation balances.

The income statement, also known as the profit and loss statement, provides a summary of a company's revenues and expenses over a specific period, such as a month, quarter, or year. The primary purpose of the income statement is to show whether the company made a profit or incurred a loss during the period. It follows the basic equation: Revenues - Expenses = Net Income.

Revenues, also known as sales or income, are the amounts earned from the company's operating activities. This includes sales of products or services and any other income generated from core business operations. For example, a retail company would report revenue from sales of merchandise, while a consulting firm would report revenue from service fees.

Expenses are the costs incurred to generate revenues and operate the business. Expenses are typically categorized into cost of goods sold (COGS) and operating expenses. COGS includes direct costs related to the production of goods or services sold, such as raw materials and direct labor. Operating expenses include all other costs required to run the business, such as salaries, rent, utilities, and marketing expenses. For instance, a manufacturing company would include the cost of raw materials and factory labor in COGS, while administrative salaries and office rent would be listed under operating expenses.

To prepare the income statement, one must first gather all revenue and expense data for the period. This involves verifying sales records, expense receipts, and other relevant financial documents. Once all data is collected, revenues are listed first, followed by COGS. The difference between revenues and COGS is the gross profit. Operating expenses are then subtracted from the gross profit to determine operating income. Any other income or expenses, such as interest or taxes, are then accounted for to arrive at the net income.

Accurate preparation of financial statements requires attention to detail and adherence to accounting principles. For instance, revenues should be recognized in the period they are earned, not necessarily when cash is received, following the accrual accounting method. Similarly, expenses should be matched with the revenues they help generate, ensuring that financial statements reflect the true economic activities of the business.

Once the balance sheet and income statement are prepared, they must be reviewed for accuracy and completeness. This involves checking for any discrepancies, ensuring that all accounts are balanced, and verifying that all transactions have been recorded correctly. Any errors or omissions should be corrected before the financial statements are finalized.

In practice, financial statements are often prepared using accounting software, which can automate many of the tasks involved and help ensure accuracy. However, even with automated systems, it is essential to understand the underlying principles and processes to interpret the results correctly and make informed decisions.

Beyond internal management purposes, financial statements are also critical for external stakeholders such as investors, creditors, and regulatory agencies. These stakeholders rely on accurate and timely financial information to assess the company's performance, make investment decisions, evaluate creditworthiness, and ensure compliance with financial reporting standards.

Understanding and preparing financial statements is crucial for individuals aiming to gain insights into a company's financial health and performance. The three primary financial statements—the income statement, the balance sheet, and the cash flow statement—each serve distinct purposes. The income statement provides a summary of a company's revenues and expenses over a specific period, demonstrating whether the company made a profit or incurred a loss. The balance sheet offers a snapshot of the company's assets, liabilities, and equity at a specific point in time. Meanwhile, the cash flow statement details the company's cash inflows and outflows over a period, highlighting how well the company manages its cash position.

To prepare an income statement, start by gathering all revenue and expense data for the period. Revenues, also known as sales or income, are the amounts earned from the company's core operating activities. For example, a retail business would report revenue from the sale of merchandise. Expenses are the costs incurred to generate those revenues, including the cost of goods sold (COGS) and operating expenses such as salaries, rent, and utilities. The difference between revenues and COGS is the gross profit, which provides a measure of the efficiency of the company's core business activities. Subtracting operating expenses from gross profit yields the operating income, which reflects the profit generated from regular business operations before accounting for non-operating items like interest and taxes. Finally, subtract other expenses and add any other income to determine the net income, or the bottom line, which indicates the overall profitability of the company for the period.

The balance sheet is organized into three main sections: assets, liabilities, and equity. Assets are resources owned by the company that are expected to bring future economic benefits. They are classified as either current or non-current, depending on their expected usage or conversion to cash within one year. Current assets include cash, accounts receivable, and inventory, while non-current assets include long-term investments, property, plant, and equipment (PP&E), and intangible assets like patents. Liabilities represent the company's obligations to creditors, also classified as current or non-current. Current liabilities include accounts payable, short-term loans, and accrued expenses, while non-current liabilities include long-term debt and deferred tax liabilities. Equity represents the owners' residual interest in the company after liabilities are deducted from assets, including items like common stock, retained earnings, and additional paid-in capital. To prepare the balance sheet, compile all relevant financial data, categorize it appropriately, and ensure the accounting equation (Assets = Liabilities + Equity) balances.

The cash flow statement is divided into three sections: operating activities, investing activities, and financing activities. The operating activities section starts with the net income from the income statement and adjusts for changes in working capital and non-cash items like depreciation and amortization. This section reflects the cash generated or used by the company's core business operations. For example, an increase in accounts receivable would be subtracted from net income, as it indicates that not all sales have been collected in cash. The investing activities section reports cash flows from the purchase and sale of long-term assets such as property, equipment, and investments. For instance, cash spent on purchasing new machinery would be included here. The financing activities section includes cash flows from transactions with the company's owners and creditors, such as issuing or repurchasing stock, borrowing, and repaying debt. For example, cash received from issuing new shares would be reported as an inflow in this section. The sum of the cash flows from these three sections equals the net change in cash for the period, which is added to the beginning cash balance to derive the ending cash balance.

Accurate preparation of these financial statements requires adherence to accounting principles and standards, such as Generally Accepted Accounting Principles (GAAP) or International Financial Reporting Standards (IFRS). These standards ensure consistency, reliability, and comparability of financial information across different companies and periods. For instance, revenue should be recognized when it is earned and realizable, regardless of when the cash is received, in accordance with the accrual basis of accounting. Similarly, expenses should be matched with the revenues they help generate, providing a more accurate picture of the company's financial performance.

The preparation process also involves making necessary adjusting entries at the end of the accounting period. These adjustments account for items such as accrued revenues, accrued expenses, and depreciation. For example, if a company has provided services but has not yet billed the customer by the end of the period, an adjusting entry is made to recognize the revenue and accounts receivable. Depreciation adjustments allocate the cost of tangible assets over their useful lives, ensuring that the expense is matched with the revenue generated by the asset.

Once the financial statements are prepared, they should be reviewed for accuracy and completeness. This involves checking for any discrepancies, ensuring that all accounts are balanced, and verifying that all transactions have been recorded correctly. Regular internal controls and audits, both internal and external, play a key role in maintaining the integrity of the financial statements. Internal controls are processes and procedures designed to ensure the accuracy and reliability of financial reporting and to safeguard the company's assets. Regular internal audits help identify any weaknesses in these controls and provide recommendations for improvement, while external audits by independent auditors offer an additional layer of assurance that the financial statements are free from material misstatement and comply with applicable accounting standards.

Adjusting entries and closing the books are essential processes in the accounting cycle that ensure financial statements accurately reflect a business's financial position and performance. These steps correct discrepancies, allocate revenues and expenses to the appropriate periods, and prepare the accounts for the new accounting period.

Consider a small consultancy firm, Bright Solutions, run by Alex. Throughout the month, Alex diligently records all financial transactions, such as client invoices, office supplies purchases, and employee salaries. However, at the end of the period, some transactions may not be fully captured in the accounts. This is where adjusting entries come into play.

Adjusting entries are made at the end of an accounting period to update account balances before financial statements are prepared. They ensure that revenues and expenses are recognized in the period they occur, adhering to the accrual basis of accounting. There are several types of adjusting entries, including accruals, deferrals, estimates, and inventory adjustments.

Accruals involve transactions where revenue has been earned or an expense has been incurred but not yet recorded. For instance, Bright Solutions completed a project for a client in December but won't receive payment until January. Alex needs to record an adjusting entry to recognize the revenue in December. This entry would debit Accounts Receivable and credit Service Revenue, ensuring the income is reflected in the correct period.

Similarly, if Bright Solutions incurs utility expenses in December but receives the bill in January, Alex must make an adjusting entry to record the expense in December. This entry would debit Utilities Expense and credit Utilities Payable. By doing so, the financial statements accurately reflect the firm's expenses, ensuring net income is correctly stated for December.

Deferrals involve transactions where cash has been received or paid in advance, but the revenue or expense pertains to a future period. For example, Bright Solutions receives an advance payment from a client for a project to be completed over the next six months. Initially, this payment is recorded as a liability in Unearned Revenue. At the end of each month, Alex makes an adjusting entry to recognize a portion of the revenue as earned. This entry would debit Unearned Revenue and credit Service Revenue, gradually transferring the amount from liability to income as the work progresses.

Prepaid expenses are another common deferral. Suppose Alex pays a year's worth of office rent in advance. Initially, this payment is recorded as an asset in Prepaid Rent. Each month, an adjusting entry is made to recognize the rent expense for that month. This entry would debit Rent Expense and credit Prepaid Rent, allocating the expense over the period it benefits.

Estimates are adjusting entries that account for items like depreciation and bad debts, where exact amounts are not known but can be reasonably estimated. Depreciation allocates the cost of a long-term asset over its useful life. If Bright Solutions purchases office equipment for $12,000, with an estimated useful life of five years, Alex needs to record monthly depreciation. This entry would debit Depreciation Expense and credit Accumulated Depreciation, spreading the cost over the asset's life.

Inventory adjustments are necessary for businesses that sell goods. They ensure the cost of goods sold and ending inventory are accurately reflected. At the end of the period, Alex conducts a physical inventory count and compares it to the recorded inventory. Any discrepancies require an adjusting entry to align the books with the actual inventory. For instance, if the physical count reveals $500 less inventory than recorded, Alex would debit Cost of Goods Sold and credit Inventory to adjust for the shortage.

Once all adjusting entries are made, Alex prepares an adjusted trial balance to verify that total debits equal total credits. This step ensures the accuracy of the accounts before preparing financial statements. The adjusted trial balance provides the basis for the income statement, balance sheet, and statement of cash flows, offering a comprehensive view of Bright Solutions' financial health.

After the financial statements are prepared and reviewed, the next step is closing the books. Closing entries zero out temporary accounts—revenues, expenses, and dividends—to transfer their balances to permanent accounts, specifically retained earnings. This process resets the temporary accounts for the new accounting period, ensuring they only reflect transactions for that period.

The closing process involves four key steps. First, revenue accounts are closed to the Income Summary account. Alex debits each revenue account and credits Income Summary for the total revenue amount. Next, expense accounts are closed to the Income Summary account. Alex debits Income Summary for the total expenses and credits each expense account.

The third step is closing the Income Summary account to Retained Earnings. The balance in the Income Summary account represents net income or loss for the period. If Bright Solutions has a net income, Alex debits Income Summary and credits Retained Earnings, increasing the equity account. Conversely, if there is a net loss, the entry would debit Retained Earnings and credit Income Summary.

Finally, dividends, if any, are closed to Retained Earnings. Alex debits Retained Earnings and credits Dividends for the total amount distributed to shareholders. This entry reduces the equity account, reflecting the payout to owners.

After closing entries are posted, Alex prepares a post-closing trial balance. This trial balance includes only the permanent accounts—assets, liabilities, and equity—ensuring that all temporary accounts have been reset to zero. The post-closing trial balance confirms that the books are in balance and ready for the new accounting period.

Imagine you're the owner of a small café called "Bean Haven." You've been running the café for a few months now, and while the day-to-day operations are running smoothly, you realize you need to get a better handle on your accounting. Understanding your financial situation is crucial for planning your future growth, managing expenses, and ensuring profitability. Here, we'll walk through practical examples and exercises to help you grasp key accounting concepts and apply them effectively to your business.

First, let's tackle recording transactions in the journal. Every time Bean Haven makes a sale, purchases supplies, or pays a bill, these transactions need to be recorded. Suppose on June 1, Bean Haven sold $500 worth of coffee and pastries. The journal entry would be:

Copy

This entry increases cash (an asset) and recognizes sales revenue. Now, suppose on the same day, you purchased $200 worth of coffee beans on credit. The journal entry would be:

Copy

This entry increases inventory (an asset) and accounts payable (a liability), reflecting that you owe money for the beans.

Next, consider adjusting entries. At the end of the month, you need to account for expenses incurred but not yet recorded or revenues earned but not yet received. Let's say it's June 30, and you need to record $100 in wages earned by your employees that haven't been paid yet. The adjusting entry would be:

Copy

This entry recognizes the expense in the period it was incurred and records the liability.

For another example, suppose you prepaid $600 for a six-month insurance policy on June 1. Initially, you recorded this as a prepaid expense:

Copy

At the end of June, you need to recognize one month of insurance expense. The adjusting entry would be:

Copy

This entry allocates one-sixth of the prepaid amount to the current period's expense.

Now, let's move on to preparing financial statements. After recording all transactions and adjustments, Bean Haven's financial position must be summarized in financial statements. The primary statements are the income statement, balance sheet, and statement of cash flows.

The income statement shows profitability over a period. For June, Bean Haven's income statement might look like this:

apache
Copy

This statement shows that Bean Haven earned $1,600 in profit for June, after accounting for all expenses.

The balance sheet provides a snapshot of financial position at a specific point in time. As of June 30, Bean Haven's balance sheet might look like this:

apache

Copy

This balance sheet shows that Bean Haven has $5,300 in assets, balanced by $700 in liabilities and $4,600 in owner's equity.

The statement of cash flows details cash inflows and outflows. For June, it might look like this:

apache

Copy

300
1 800

500
500

1 200
1 200

2 500
0
2 500

This statement shows how Bean Haven's cash position changed during June, highlighting cash generated from operating activities, investments made, and contributions received from the owner. This comprehensive view helps you understand where your cash comes from and how it is used, essential for managing liquidity.

500
500

Introduction to Cost Accounting

Cost accounting is a vital tool for businesses of all sizes, providing essential insights into where money is spent, how resources are utilized, and how costs can be controlled. Unlike financial accounting, which focuses on creating financial statements for external stakeholders, cost accounting is primarily used internally by management to make informed decisions. Understanding the principles and techniques of cost accounting can significantly enhance a company's efficiency and profitability.

At its core, cost accounting involves the recording, analysis, and allocation of costs associated with the production of goods or services. This process starts with the identification of various types of costs. Broadly, costs can be classified into direct and indirect costs. Direct costs are those that can be directly traced to a product, such as raw materials and labor. For instance, in a furniture manufacturing company, the wood used to create a table and the wages paid to the carpenters assembling it are direct costs. Indirect costs, on the other hand, cannot be directly traced to a single product and often include items like factory rent, utilities, and administrative salaries. These costs must be allocated across different products or departments using appropriate methods.

One of the fundamental techniques in cost accounting is job order costing. This method is used when products are produced based on specific customer orders, and each product can be individually identified. A custom furniture maker, for instance, would use job order costing. In this system, costs are accumulated for each job separately. Materials, labor, and overhead costs are tracked as they are incurred, and at the completion of the job, the total cost is calculated. This method provides detailed cost information and helps in setting the price for each job.

Another widely used method is process costing, suitable for industries where products are indistinguishable from each other, such as chemicals, beverages, or paper. In process costing, costs are assigned to each process or department. For example, in a beverage manufacturing company, the production process might include mixing, bottling, and packaging departments. Costs are accumulated for each department over a period and then averaged over all units produced, providing an average cost per unit. This method helps in understanding the cost structure of each production stage and in identifying areas for cost reduction.

Activity-based costing (ABC) is a more refined approach that allocates overhead costs based on the activities that drive those costs. Unlike traditional costing methods that might allocate overhead uniformly, ABC recognizes that different products consume resources differently. For instance, in a manufacturing company, machine setups, inspections, and material handling are activities that incur costs. ABC assigns costs to products based on the number of activities required to produce them. This method provides more accurate product cost information and helps in identifying inefficient processes.

Standard costing involves setting predetermined costs for products and services, which are then compared with actual costs. Variances between standard and actual costs are analyzed to identify areas where performance is not meeting expectations. For example, if the standard cost to produce a widget is $5 but the actual cost is $6, the $1 variance needs to be investigated. It could be due to higher material prices, inefficient labor, or machine downtime. Standard costing aids in budgeting, performance evaluation, and cost control.

Marginal costing, or variable costing, considers only variable costs—those that change with the level of production—when calculating the cost of a product. Fixed costs, such as rent and salaries, are treated as period costs and are not included in product cost calculations. This method is useful for decision-making, particularly in scenarios like pricing, product mix, and make-or-buy decisions. For instance, if a company has excess capacity, knowing the marginal cost can help in pricing products competitively without affecting overall profitability.

Cost-volume-profit (CVP) analysis is another critical tool in cost accounting that helps in understanding the relationship between cost, volume, and profit. It involves calculating the break-even point—the level of sales at which total revenues equal total costs, resulting in zero profit. Beyond this point, every unit sold contributes to profit. CVP analysis assists in making crucial decisions like setting sales targets, determining the impact of changes in costs or prices, and planning for different levels of production.

Budgeting is an integral part of cost accounting, providing a financial plan for the future. Budgets set targets for revenues, costs, and profits, and serve as a benchmark for performance evaluation. Various types of budgets, such as operating budgets, capital budgets, and cash flow budgets, help in planning and controlling different aspects of business operations. For instance, an operating budget outlines expected revenues and expenses for a specific period, guiding day-to-day operations and ensuring that resources are used efficiently.

Variance analysis, a follow-up to budgeting, involves comparing actual performance with budgeted figures and analyzing the reasons for any deviations. Positive variances indicate better-than-expected performance, while negative variances signal problems that need to be addressed. For example, if actual material costs are higher than budgeted, it might indicate issues with supplier pricing or material wastage. By identifying and understanding variances, management can take corrective actions to improve future performance.

Cost accounting also plays a crucial role in strategic decision-making, helping managers evaluate the financial implications of various strategic options. For instance, when considering whether to enter a new market, introduce a new product, or discontinue an existing product line, cost accounting provides detailed insights into the potential costs and benefits. Techniques such as cost-benefit analysis, which compares the expected costs of an action to its anticipated benefits, are used to support these decisions. For example, if a company is evaluating the introduction of a new product, cost accounting helps in estimating the development, production, marketing, and distribution costs and comparing them to the projected revenue.

Types of Costs: Fixed, Variable, and Mixed

Understanding the different types of costs is crucial for effective financial management and decision-making in any business. Costs can be broadly categorized into fixed, variable, and mixed costs, each playing a distinct role in the company's financial structure. Recognizing how these costs behave under various conditions helps managers plan budgets, set prices, and control spending more efficiently.

Fixed costs are expenses that do not change with the level of production or sales activity within a certain range. These costs remain constant regardless of how much a company produces or sells. Examples of fixed costs include rent, salaries of permanent employees, insurance, and depreciation of assets. For instance, consider a bakery that rents space for $2,000 per month. This rental cost remains the same whether the bakery produces 100 loaves of bread or 1,000. Fixed costs are essential to cover because they must be paid irrespective of business performance, making them a stable but potentially burdensome part of financial planning.

The constancy of fixed costs provides stability in financial forecasting. However, they can also impose significant stress during periods of low sales or production. For example, during an economic downturn, a business must still cover its fixed costs even if revenue drops, potentially squeezing profit margins. This characteristic underscores the importance of maintaining a balance between fixed and variable costs to enhance financial flexibility.

Variable costs, in contrast, fluctuate with the level of production or sales. These costs are directly proportional to the volume of goods produced or services rendered. Common examples of variable costs include raw materials, direct labor (wages for workers directly involved in production), and sales commissions. For instance, if a clothing manufacturer pays $5 for each piece of fabric and produces 200 shirts, the total cost of fabric will be $1,000. If production increases to 500 shirts, the fabric cost rises to $2,500. This direct correlation between production volume and cost makes variable costs easier to manage during fluctuations in business activity.

Variable costs offer flexibility because they align with business performance. During periods of high demand, variable costs increase but are offset by higher revenue. Conversely, during slower periods, variable costs decrease, helping to mitigate financial strain. This adaptability is beneficial for businesses with seasonal variations in sales or those operating in highly competitive markets where production volumes can change rapidly.

Mixed costs, also known as semi-variable or semi-fixed costs, contain elements of both fixed and variable costs. These costs have a fixed component that remains constant regardless of activity level, and a variable component that changes with the level of production or sales. A typical example is a utility bill, which may have a fixed base charge plus a variable charge based on usage. For instance, a manufacturing plant might have a fixed monthly electricity charge of $500, plus an additional $0.10 per kilowatt-hour of electricity used. If the plant uses 3,000 kilowatt-hours in a month, the total electricity cost would be $800 ($500 fixed + $300 variable).

Understanding mixed costs is important because they require a different approach to budgeting and cost control. The fixed component needs to be covered regardless of business activity, while the variable component must be managed based on production levels. Analyzing mixed costs often involves separating the fixed and variable elements for better financial planning. For example, using historical data and statistical methods like regression analysis, a company can determine the fixed and variable portions of its mixed costs, enabling more accurate forecasting and budgeting.

In the context of pricing strategies, knowing the composition of costs is essential. Cost-plus pricing, for example, involves adding a markup to the total cost of producing a product to ensure a profit margin. To apply this method accurately, a business must distinguish between fixed and variable costs to calculate the total cost precisely. If a company misclassifies costs, it might set prices too low, resulting in losses, or too high, reducing competitiveness. For instance, a company producing handcrafted furniture must consider both the fixed costs of its workshop and the variable costs of materials and labor. By accurately accounting for these costs, the company can set a price that covers costs and provides a profit margin.

Cost allocation and absorption costing are fundamental concepts in managerial accounting, essential for accurately determining the costs associated with producing goods or services. Imagine a small manufacturing company, "EcoCraft Furniture," which specializes in custom-made, eco-friendly furniture. As the owner, you need to understand how to allocate costs effectively to ensure your products are priced competitively while maintaining profitability.

Cost allocation is the process of identifying, aggregating, and assigning costs to cost objects such as products, departments, or projects. In EcoCraft Furniture, you have various costs like raw materials, labor, and overheads that need to be allocated to the different types of furniture you produce. Consider direct costs, which are easily traceable to a specific product, and indirect costs, which need to be allocated based on a rational method.

Direct costs include items like wood, varnish, and labor directly involved in crafting each piece of furniture. For instance, if a custom dining table requires $200 worth of wood and $50 worth of varnish, these costs are directly assigned to that table. Additionally, if an employee spends 10 hours working on the table at a rate of $20 per hour, the direct labor cost is $200.

Indirect costs, such as utilities, rent, and administrative salaries, require a more nuanced approach. These costs cannot be directly traced to a single product, so they need to be allocated using a systematic method. One common approach is to use a predetermined overhead rate based on direct labor hours or machine hours. Suppose your total estimated overhead costs for the year are $100,000, and you expect to use 10,000 direct labor hours. The overhead rate would be $10 per labor hour.

Applying this rate, if the dining table took 10 hours to produce, you would allocate $100 of overhead to it. Summarizing the costs, the total cost for the dining table would be:

Direct materials: $250

Direct labor: $200

Overhead: $100

Total cost: $550

Absorption costing, also known as full costing, is a method where all manufacturing costs, both fixed and variable, are absorbed by the units produced. This method ensures that each unit of product carries its share of the fixed manufacturing overhead, thus providing a more comprehensive view of product costs.

To illustrate, let's extend our example with EcoCraft Furniture. Suppose your fixed manufacturing overhead includes $50,000 for factory rent and $20,000 for equipment depreciation annually. If you plan to produce 1,000 units of furniture in a year, the fixed overhead per unit would be:

Factory rent per unit: $50 ($50,000 / 1,000 units)

Equipment depreciation per unit: $20 ($20,000 / 1,000 units)

Total fixed overhead per unit: $70

Now, let's incorporate this into the total cost of the dining table:

Direct materials: $250

Direct labor: $200

Variable overhead: $100

Fixed overhead: $70

Total cost per unit (absorption costing): $620

Absorption costing ensures that all production costs are included in the cost per unit, which helps in setting prices that cover all expenses and contribute to profitability. This method is also required for external financial reporting, as it aligns with Generally Accepted Accounting Principles (GAAP).

However, absorption costing can sometimes obscure the impact of fixed costs on profitability, especially when production levels fluctuate. To address this, consider variable costing (or direct costing), which only assigns variable manufacturing costs to products, treating fixed overhead as a period expense. While variable costing provides clearer insights into the impact of production volume on profitability, it is not permissible for external financial reporting.

Returning to EcoCraft Furniture, imagine a scenario where you experience a drop in demand, and you only produce 800 units instead of the planned 1,000. Under absorption costing, the fixed overhead per unit increases because the total fixed costs are spread over fewer units:

Factory rent per unit: $62.50 ($50,000 / 800 units)

Equipment depreciation per unit: $25 ($20,000 / 800 units)

Total fixed overhead per unit: $87.50

The new total cost for the dining table would be:

Direct materials: $250

Direct labor: $200

Variable overhead: $100

Fixed overhead: $87.50

Total cost per unit (adjusted for lower production): $637.50

This demonstrates how absorption costing can affect cost per unit with changes in production volume, highlighting the importance of maintaining stable production levels to control unit costs.

For managerial decision-making, understanding both absorption and variable costing can provide valuable insights. For example, during periods of low demand, you might consider strategies to reduce fixed costs or increase production efficiency to manage unit costs effectively. Alternatively, variable costing can help in pricing decisions, cost control, and performance evaluation by isolating the variable costs directly tied to production.

In practice, cost allocation methods can vary, and choosing the right method depends on the nature of your business and the specifics of your production processes. Different methods of cost allocation include:

Direct Allocation Method: This method assigns costs directly to a cost object without any intermediate cost pools. It is straightforward but may not be suitable for complex operations with multiple indirect costs.

Step-Down Method: This method allocates costs from service departments to production departments in a sequential manner. It considers the mutual services rendered among service departments, providing a more refined approach than the direct allocation method.

Activity-Based Costing (ABC): ABC allocates overhead costs based on activities that drive costs, such as machine setups, inspections, or material handling. It provides a more accurate cost per product by identifying the actual activities and their associated costs.

For EcoCraft Furniture, let's consider implementing Activity-Based Costing. Assume you identify three main activities that drive overhead costs: machine setups, quality inspections, and material handling. The total overhead costs and cost drivers are estimated as follows:

Machine setups: $30,000, driven by 150 setups

Quality inspections: $40,000, driven by 400 inspections

Material handling: $30,000, driven by 1,000 material moves

The cost per activity would be:

Machine setup cost per activity: $200 ($30,000 / 150 setups)

Quality inspection cost per activity: $100 ($40,000 / 400 inspections)

Material handling cost per activity: $30 ($30,000 / 1,000 material moves)

Now, let's allocate these costs to the dining table. Suppose producing a dining table involves 1 machine setup, 3 quality inspections, and 5 material moves. The allocated overhead would be:

Machine setup: $200 (1 setup x $200)

Quality inspections: $300 (3 inspections x $100)

Material handling: $150 (5 moves x $30)

Total ABC overhead: $650

Adding these to the direct costs, the total cost of the dining table using ABC would be:

Direct materials: $250

Direct labor: $200

ABC overhead: $650

Total cost per unit (ABC): $1,100

Activity-Based Costing shows a significantly higher overhead allocation compared to traditional absorption costing, reflecting the true cost of production activities. This detailed costing can help EcoCraft Furniture better understand cost drivers and identify areas for efficiency improvements.

Effective cost allocation and absorption costing not only ensure accurate product costing but also support strategic decision-making. For example, by analyzing ABC data, EcoCraft Furniture might find that machine setups are particularly costly, prompting an investment in more efficient equipment or process changes to reduce setup times.

Additionally, understanding the full cost structure enables better pricing strategies. With accurate cost data, you can set prices that cover all costs and ensure a desired profit margin. For instance, if the market price for a custom dining table is $1,500, knowing that the total cost is $1,100 (as per ABC) helps in setting a competitive yet profitable price.

Moreover, accurate cost allocation supports budgeting and financial planning. By understanding the fixed and variable components of your costs, you can forecast future expenses more accurately, plan for capital investments, and manage cash flow effectively. For example, during a period of anticipated demand increase, you might plan for additional labor or equipment to meet production needs without incurring excessive costs.

Cost allocation and absorption costing also play a crucial role in performance evaluation. By comparing actual costs to budgeted costs, you can identify variances and investigate their causes. For instance, if actual material costs are consistently higher than budgeted, it may indicate inefficiencies in procurement or production processes that need to be addressed.

In conclusion, mastering cost allocation and absorption costing is essential for managing a business effectively. These methods ensure that all costs are accurately captured and assigned to products, providing a clear picture of profitability and cost drivers. For EcoCraft Furniture, implementing these practices can lead to better pricing decisions, improved efficiency, and enhanced financial planning. By understanding and applying these concepts, you can ensure your business is well-positioned for sustainable growth and success.

Budgeting and Variance Analysis

Budgeting and variance analysis are fundamental components of effective financial management. They serve as the backbone for planning, controlling, and evaluating an organization's financial performance. By creating detailed budgets and conducting thorough variance analyses, businesses can ensure they stay on track to meet their financial goals, adapt to changing conditions, and make informed decisions.

Imagine a small manufacturing company, Precision Tools, that recently expanded its product line. To manage this growth, the company needed a robust budgeting process to allocate resources efficiently and track financial performance. The first step in this process was to create a comprehensive budget. This involved estimating revenues, costs, and expenses for the upcoming fiscal year. Precision Tools began by analyzing historical financial data, considering market trends, and incorporating input from various departments.

The revenue budget was a critical component. It required forecasting sales for each product line, taking into account seasonal variations and market demand. Precision Tools used a combination of historical sales data and market research to project future revenues. This step was crucial, as accurate revenue forecasts would influence other budget components, such as production costs and marketing expenses.

Next, the company developed its production budget. This involved determining the quantity of each product to be manufactured, considering both forecasted sales and inventory levels. Precision Tools needed to ensure that production levels matched demand without leading to excess inventory or stockouts. The production budget included estimates for direct materials, labor, and overhead costs. By carefully planning these elements, Precision Tools aimed to optimize its production processes and control costs.

The operating budget included all other expenses necessary to run the business, such as administrative costs, marketing expenses, and research and development. Precision Tools allocated funds for each department, ensuring that all areas had the resources needed to achieve their goals. This comprehensive approach helped the company maintain a clear picture of its financial commitments and avoid overspending.

Once the budget was established, Precision Tools implemented a system for monitoring and controlling its financial performance. This is where variance analysis came into play. Variance analysis involves comparing actual financial results to budgeted figures and identifying deviations. By regularly conducting variance analyses, Precision Tools could pinpoint areas where performance differed from expectations and take corrective actions.

For instance, suppose Precision Tools budgeted $100,000 for raw materials in a given month, but actual spending was $120,000. The $20,000 difference is a variance that needs to be investigated. Variance analysis helps determine the root causes of such discrepancies, which can include factors like price fluctuations, inefficient use of materials, or errors in forecasting.

To facilitate variance analysis, Precision Tools set up a system to regularly track and report financial performance. Monthly financial statements were prepared, comparing actual results to the budget. These statements included detailed breakdowns of revenues, costs, and expenses, allowing managers to identify variances quickly. By involving department heads in the review process, the company ensured that everyone was accountable for their areas and could provide insights into variances.

In one instance, the marketing department noticed a significant variance in advertising expenses. The budget allocated $15,000 for a particular campaign, but actual spending reached $25,000. Upon investigation, it was discovered that the additional costs were due to an unanticipated increase in advertising rates. The marketing team provided this information to management, who then adjusted the budget for future campaigns to reflect the new rates. This proactive approach helped the company maintain control over its marketing expenses and avoid similar variances in the future.

Another example involved the production department, which reported a variance in labor costs. The budget estimated $50,000 for labor in a given quarter, but actual costs were $60,000. A detailed analysis revealed that the variance was due to overtime hours needed to meet an unexpected surge in demand. Understanding this allowed Precision Tools to evaluate its staffing levels and consider hiring additional workers to minimize overtime costs in the future.

Variance analysis also played a crucial role in identifying positive variances, where actual results exceeded budgeted expectations. For example, if the company budgeted $200,000 in sales for a month but achieved $250,000, the $50,000 positive variance indicated strong performance. By examining the factors contributing to this success, such as effective marketing strategies or increased market demand, Precision Tools could replicate these practices in future periods.

To make variance analysis more actionable, Precision Tools categorized variances into two main types: favorable and unfavorable. Favorable variances occurred when actual results were better than budgeted figures, such as higher revenues or lower costs. Unfavorable variances occurred when actual results fell short of budgeted figures, such as lower revenues or higher costs. This categorization helped management prioritize which variances required immediate attention and which ones presented opportunities for further improvement.

Effective variance analysis requires not only identifying variances but also taking corrective actions. Precision Tools established a process for addressing significant variances promptly. When an unfavorable variance was identified, the responsible department head worked with their team to develop an action plan. This plan included steps to investigate the root cause, implement corrective measures, and monitor the results. By addressing variances proactively, Precision Tools minimized their impact on overall financial performance.

For instance , when the production department identified the overtime costs as a significant unfavorable variance, they developed a plan to mitigate this issue. They analyzed the root causes of increased overtime and concluded that hiring additional part-time workers during peak demand periods would be more cost-effective than relying on overtime. This strategy was implemented in the next production cycle, and future variance reports showed a reduction in overtime costs, aligning closer with the budgeted figures.

Case Study: Implementing Cost Controls in a Small Business

Nestled in a bustling downtown area, The Green Thumb, a small but thriving plant nursery, faced mounting financial pressures despite steady sales. Owner Emily Sanchez was determined to get a handle on her finances and ensure the long-term viability of her business. This case study explores how Emily successfully implemented cost controls to stabilize her nursery's financial health.

Emily's journey began with a detailed financial audit of The Green Thumb. She meticulously reviewed her income statements, balance sheets, and cash flow statements to understand where her money was going. This initial audit revealed several areas of concern: high overhead costs, fluctuating utility bills, and inconsistent supply expenses. Armed with this data, Emily knew she needed a strategic approach to implement effective cost controls.

One of the first steps Emily took was to address her fixed costs. Rent, a significant portion of her overhead, was non-negotiable in the short term, but she found room for negotiation in other areas. For instance, she renegotiated her insurance premiums, which had been steadily increasing over the years. By comparing quotes from different providers and demonstrating her company's solid track record, Emily secured a lower premium, saving several hundred dollars annually.

Next, Emily turned her attention to variable costs, particularly those related to supplies and inventory. She realized that purchasing in bulk could yield significant savings. However, limited storage space meant she had to be strategic about which items to buy in larger quantities. Emily analyzed her sales data to identify high-turnover products and negotiated bulk purchase agreements with suppliers for these items. This not only reduced costs per unit but also ensured she always had popular items in stock, boosting customer satisfaction and sales.

Seasonality played a significant role in The Green Thumb's utility expenses, with heating costs soaring in winter and cooling costs spiking in summer. Emily decided to invest in energy-efficient solutions. She installed programmable thermostats to better control heating and cooling, replaced old insulation, and switched to LED lighting throughout the nursery. These changes required an upfront investment, but the long-term savings on utility bills were substantial, quickly offsetting the initial costs.

Labor costs were another area where Emily saw potential for savings. She introduced a flexible staffing model, hiring part-time employees during peak seasons and scaling back during slower months. To ensure operational efficiency, she cross-trained her staff, allowing them to take on multiple roles as needed. This approach not only reduced labor costs but also improved employee morale by providing varied work experiences.

Emily also implemented a more rigorous inventory management system. Previously, she had relied on manual counts and ad-hoc ordering, leading to overstocking and occasional shortages. She adopted inventory management software that provided real-time tracking and automated reorder alerts. This system helped her maintain optimal stock levels, reducing wastage from perishable items and ensuring that popular products were always available.

To further tighten cost controls, Emily scrutinized her marketing expenses. She shifted from traditional advertising methods, such as print ads and flyers, to more cost-effective digital marketing strategies. By leveraging social media platforms and email marketing, she reached a broader audience at a fraction of the cost. Additionally, Emily partnered with local businesses for cross-promotional campaigns, sharing marketing expenses and tapping into new customer bases.

Recognizing the importance of continuous improvement, Emily established a monthly review process. Each month, she and her team analyzed financial reports, comparing actual expenses against budgets and identifying any variances. This proactive approach allowed them to address issues promptly, ensuring that cost controls remained effective and aligned with business goals.

Emily's efforts to implement cost controls at The Green Thumb yielded impressive results. Within a year, she had reduced overall expenses by 15%, significantly improving the nursery's profitability. These savings allowed her to reinvest in the business, expanding her product range and enhancing the customer experience. For example, she used some of the savings to create a cozy seating area where customers could relax and enjoy their new plants, a feature that became a popular draw.

Moreover, Emily's approach fostered a culture of cost consciousness among her staff. Employees became more mindful of resource usage, from turning off lights in unused areas to minimizing waste in daily operations. This collective effort further contributed to the nursery's financial health and sustainability.

Emily's story highlights several key principles of effective cost control for small businesses. First, a thorough understanding of financials is crucial. By conducting a detailed audit, Emily identified specific areas where costs could be reduced. Second, negotiation and strategic purchasing can yield significant savings. Emily's efforts to renegotiate insurance premiums and buy supplies in bulk are testament to this. Third, investing in efficiency can lead to long-term savings. Emily's energy-efficient upgrades and inventory management system are prime examples.

Another critical lesson from Emily's experience is the importance of flexibility and adaptability in labor management. By adjusting staffing levels based on seasonal demand and cross-training employees, she optimized labor costs while maintaining high service standards. Additionally, embracing digital marketing and forming strategic partnerships proved to be cost-effective ways to reach new customers and boost sales.

Finally, Emily's commitment to continuous monitoring and improvement ensured that cost controls remained effective over time. Regular financial reviews allowed her to stay on top of her expenses and make adjustments as needed, fostering a proactive rather than reactive approach to financial management.

Chapter 4: Financial Analysis for Decision-Making

Financial Ratios and Metrics

Understanding financial ratios and metrics is crucial for anyone looking to manage a business effectively. These tools provide valuable insights into a company's performance, financial health, and operational efficiency. By mastering financial ratios and metrics, you can make informed decisions that drive growth and profitability.

At the heart of financial analysis are several key ratios that fall into different categories: liquidity ratios, profitability ratios, leverage ratios, efficiency ratios, and market value ratios. Each category offers a unique perspective on the business, helping to pinpoint strengths, weaknesses, and potential areas for improvement.

Liquidity ratios measure a company's ability to meet its short-term obligations. The most commonly used liquidity ratios are the current ratio and the quick ratio. The current ratio is calculated by dividing current assets by current liabilities. A current ratio above 1 indicates that the company has more current assets than current liabilities, suggesting good short-term financial health. However, a very high ratio might indicate that the company is not efficiently using its assets.

The quick ratio, also known as the acid-test ratio, refines the current ratio by excluding inventory from current assets. This ratio is calculated by dividing quick assets (current assets minus inventory) by current liabilities. The quick ratio provides a more stringent test of liquidity, as it focuses on the most liquid assets. A quick ratio above 1 is generally considered satisfactory, indicating that the company can cover its short-term obligations without relying on the sale of inventory.

Profitability ratios assess a company's ability to generate profit relative to its revenue, assets, equity, and other financial metrics. Key profitability ratios include the gross profit margin, operating profit margin, net profit margin, return on assets (ROA), and return on equity (ROE). The gross profit margin, calculated by dividing gross profit by revenue, indicates how efficiently a company is producing its goods. A higher gross profit margin suggests better efficiency in production and cost control.

The operating profit margin, derived from dividing operating income by revenue, measures the proportion of revenue left after covering operating expenses. This ratio highlights the company's operational efficiency and its ability to generate profit from its core business activities. The net profit margin, calculated by dividing net income by revenue, shows the overall profitability after all expenses, including taxes and interest, have been deducted. A higher net profit margin indicates a more profitable company.

Return on assets (ROA) and return on equity (ROE) are essential for evaluating how effectively a company uses its assets and equity to generate profit. ROA is calculated by dividing net income by total assets, providing insight into how efficiently the company is managing its assets. ROE, derived from dividing net income by shareholders' equity, measures the return generated on the shareholders' investment. Both ratios are crucial for assessing management's effectiveness and the company's overall financial performance.

Leverage ratios, also known as solvency ratios, examine a company's use of debt to finance its operations and growth. The debt-to-equity ratio, calculated by dividing total debt by shareholders' equity, indicates the proportion of debt financing relative to equity financing. A higher debt-to-equity ratio suggests greater financial leverage, which can amplify returns but also increase financial risk. The interest coverage ratio, derived from dividing operating income by interest expense, measures the company's ability to meet its interest obligations.

A higher ratio indicates greater ease in meeting interest payments, suggesting better financial stability.

Efficiency ratios evaluate how well a company utilizes its assets and manages its operations. Key efficiency ratios include inventory turnover, accounts receivable turnover, and accounts payable turnover. Inventory turnover, calculated by dividing cost of goods sold by average inventory, measures how quickly a company sells its inventory. A higher inventory turnover indicates efficient inventory management and strong sales. Conversely, a low turnover might suggest overstocking or weak sales.

Accounts receivable turnover, derived from dividing net credit sales by average accounts receivable, assesses how effectively a company collects payments from its customers. A higher turnover ratio indicates efficient credit and collections processes, while a lower ratio might suggest issues with credit policies or customer payment delays. Accounts payable turnover, calculated by dividing cost of goods sold by average accounts payable, measures how quickly a company pays its suppliers. A higher ratio indicates prompt payments, which can enhance supplier relationships, while a lower ratio might suggest cash flow challenges or extended payment terms.

Market value ratios provide insights into a company's stock market performance and investor perceptions. Key market value ratios include the price-to-earnings (P/E) ratio, price-to-book (P/B) ratio, and dividend yield. The P/E ratio, calculated by dividing the market price per share by earnings per share (EPS), indicates how much investors are willing to pay for each dollar of earnings. A higher P/E ratio suggests higher growth expectations, while a lower ratio might indicate undervaluation or lower growth prospects.

The P/B ratio, derived from dividing the market price per share by book value per share, measures the market's valuation relative to the company's net asset value. A higher P/B ratio indicates that investors expect high future growth, while a lower ratio might suggest undervaluation or concerns about the company's prospects. Dividend yield, calculated by

Understanding financial ratios and metrics is crucial for anyone looking to manage a business effectively. These tools provide valuable insights into a company's performance, financial health, and operational efficiency. By mastering financial ratios and metrics, you can make informed decisions that drive growth and profitability.

Interpreting Financial Statements for Business Insights

Interpreting financial statements is akin to reading the vital signs of a business. These documents provide the necessary insights to gauge the health, performance, and potential of any enterprise. Imagine you're at the helm of a burgeoning tech startup called "Innovatech." Understanding your financial statements can mean the difference between strategic growth and unforeseen pitfalls.

The balance sheet, income statement, and cash flow statement are the three primary financial documents you'll encounter. Each serves a unique purpose and together, they present a comprehensive view of your company's financial status.

The balance sheet offers a snapshot of Innovatech's financial position at a given moment. It's divided into three main sections: assets, liabilities, and equity. Assets are what your company owns, such as cash, inventory, and equipment. Liabilities represent what your company owes, including loans, accounts payable, and mortgages. Equity, also known as shareholders' equity, is the residual interest in the assets of the entity after deducting liabilities. The fundamental equation here is:

$$\text{Assets} = \text{Liabilities} + \text{Equity} \quad \text{Assets} = \text{Liabilities} + \text{Equity}$$

Imagine Innovatech's balance sheet shows total assets of $500,000, total liabilities of $200,000, and equity of $300,000. This indicates a strong equity position, suggesting that the company is well-capitalized and has a cushion to absorb potential losses.

The income statement, also known as the profit and loss statement, details Innovatech's performance over a specific period, usually a quarter or a year. It starts with revenue and subtracts expenses to determine the net profit or loss. Key components include revenue, cost of goods sold (COGS), gross profit, operating expenses, and net income. For instance, if Innovatech generated $1 million in revenue, had $400,000 in COGS, and $300,000 in operating expenses, the income statement would look like this:

Revenue: $1,000,000

COGS: $400,000

Gross Profit: $600,000

Operating Expenses: $300,000

Net Income: $300,000

This income statement tells you that Innovatech is profitable, with a healthy gross profit margin of 60% and a net profit margin of 30%. These margins are crucial for assessing operational efficiency and profitability.

The cash flow statement tracks the flow of cash in and out of Innovatech over a period. It's divided into three sections: operating activities, investing activities, and financing activities. Operating activities include cash transactions related to core business operations, such as receipts from sales and payments to suppliers. Investing activities cover cash used for investments in assets like equipment or other companies. Financing activities encompass borrowing and repaying loans, issuing stock, and paying dividends.

Suppose Innovatech's cash flow statement shows $200,000 net cash from operating activities, -$50,000 net cash from investing activities, and $100,000 net cash from financing activities. This results in a net increase in cash of $250,000. Such a positive cash flow indicates that Innovatech is generating sufficient cash from its operations to invest in growth and manage its financing needs.

Interpreting these financial statements involves more than just reading numbers. It requires analyzing trends, ratios, and comparisons to derive meaningful insights. Financial ratios are powerful tools in this analysis. Let's explore some key ratios and how they can provide deeper insights into Innovatech's financial health.

The current ratio, calculated as current assets divided by current liabilities, measures liquidity. A ratio above 1 indicates that the company can cover its short-term obligations. For instance, if Innovatech has $300,000 in current assets and $150,000 in current liabilities, the current ratio is 2.0, suggesting strong liquidity.

The debt-to-equity ratio, calculated as total liabilities divided by shareholders' equity, assesses financial leverage. A lower ratio implies less reliance on debt for financing. If Innovatech has $200,000 in liabilities and $300,000 in equity, the debt-to-equity ratio is 0.67, indicating a balanced approach to leveraging debt.

Profitability ratios like the gross margin, operating margin, and net margin provide insights into operational efficiency. The gross margin, calculated as (revenue - COGS) / revenue, shows the percentage of revenue remaining after covering the cost of goods sold. For Innovatech, with a gross profit of $600,000 and revenue of $1,000,000, the gross margin is 60%. This high margin suggests effective cost control in production.

The operating margin, calculated as operating income divided by revenue, evaluates the efficiency of core business operations. With an operating income of $300,000, Innovatech's operating margin is 30%, indicating strong operational efficiency. The net margin, calculated as net income divided by revenue, reflects overall profitability. Innovatech's net margin is also 30%, reinforcing its profitability.

Efficiency ratios, such as inventory turnover and accounts receivable turnover, measure how effectively Innovatech is managing its assets. Inventory turnover is calculated as COGS divided by average inventory. If Innovatech's COGS is $400,000 and its average inventory is $50,000, the inventory turnover ratio is 8. This means Innovatech sells and replaces its inventory eight times a year, indicating efficient inventory management.

Break-even analysis and marginal costing are fundamental concepts in managerial accounting that provide crucial insights for decision-making. Imagine you're running a small bakery, "Heavenly Bakes," and you're trying to determine the point at which your business becomes profitable. This is where break-even analysis comes into play.

The break-even point is the level of sales at which total revenues equal total costs, resulting in neither profit nor loss. Understanding this point helps you make informed pricing, production, and investment decisions. To calculate the break-even point, you need to know your fixed costs, variable costs per unit, and the selling price per unit.

Fixed costs are expenses that do not change with the level of production or sales, such as rent, salaries, and insurance. For Heavenly Bakes, these might include the monthly lease for your bakery space and the salaries of your staff. Variable costs, on the other hand, vary directly with production volume. This could include ingredients like flour, sugar, and eggs, as well as packaging materials.

To illustrate, let's say Heavenly Bakes has fixed costs of $5,000 per month. Each loaf of bread costs $2 in variable costs, and you sell each loaf for $5. The contribution margin per unit, which is the selling price minus the variable cost per unit, is $3. The break-even point in units can be calculated using the formula:

Break-
even point (units)=Fixed CostsSelling Price per Unit−Variable Cost per UnitBrea
k-even point (units)=Selling Price per Unit−Variable Cost per UnitFixed Costs

In this case:

Break-even point=50005−2=50003≈1667Break-even point=5−25000=35000≈1667

This means you need to sell approximately 1,667 loaves of bread each month to cover all your costs. Any sales beyond this point contribute to profit.

Now, let's delve into marginal costing, another critical concept. Marginal costing, also known as variable costing or direct costing, focuses on the cost of producing one additional unit of a product. This method considers only variable costs in decision-making, ignoring fixed costs which are treated as period costs and deducted from total contribution to arrive at net profit.

In practice, marginal costing is invaluable for pricing decisions, optimizing production levels, and analyzing profitability. For instance, if Heavenly Bakes is considering introducing a new product, such as a specialty cake, marginal costing helps determine the minimum price at which the cake should be sold to cover its variable costs.

Assume the variable cost of making one specialty cake is $10. Using marginal costing, you can decide if it's feasible to sell the cake at a certain price point. If the market suggests a price of $15 per cake, the contribution margin would be $5. As long as this contribution margin is positive and sufficient to cover your fixed costs in the long run, introducing the specialty cake could be a profitable decision.

Marginal costing also aids in decision-making when faced with special orders. Suppose a corporate client offers to buy 500 loaves of bread at a discounted price of $4 per loaf. At first glance, this seems lower than your usual selling price. However, using marginal costing, you focus on the contribution margin. Since the variable cost per loaf is $2, selling at $4 still provides a contribution of $2 per loaf. If this special order doesn't affect your regular sales and covers the variable costs, it can be accepted as it contributes to covering fixed costs and potentially increasing profit.

Moreover, marginal costing assists in evaluating make-or-buy decisions. Consider Heavenly Bakes contemplating whether to bake its own pastries or outsource them. By comparing the variable cost of baking in-house with the purchase cost from an external supplier, you can make an informed decision. If baking in-house costs $3 per pastry in variable costs and the supplier offers them at $4 each, marginal costing suggests baking in-house is more cost-effective unless other qualitative factors override the cost difference.

Break-even analysis and marginal costing also play a role in managing capacity and production decisions. For instance, if Heavenly Bakes operates at full capacity and faces a decision to expand or outsource, marginal costing helps assess the additional costs and benefits. If the marginal cost of increasing production is lower than the revenue from additional sales, expansion might be justified.

However, these concepts are not without limitations. Break-even analysis assumes that fixed and variable costs are constant, which might not hold true in the real world where costs can fluctuate. Marginal costing, while useful for short-term decisions, doesn't provide a complete picture for long-term strategic planning as it ignores fixed costs in decision-making.

To mitigate these limitations, it's essential to integrate break-even analysis and marginal costing with other financial and non-financial metrics. For example, combining these tools with market analysis, competitor pricing, and customer demand trends provides a more holistic view. Regularly revisiting and updating cost assumptions ensures that the analysis remains relevant and accurate.

Furthermore, sensitivity analysis enhances the robustness of these tools by examining how changes in key variables—such as selling price, variable costs, and fixed costs—affect the break-even point and profitability. For instance, you could create different scenarios for Heavenly Bakes, such as a 10% increase in ingredient costs or a new competitor entering the market, to see how these changes impact your financial outcomes. This proactive approach allows you to prepare for potential challenges and make informed strategic decisions.

Forecasting and financial planning are essential processes for ensuring a business's long-term success. They involve predicting future financial performance and creating strategies to achieve desired financial outcomes. Both practices require a blend of analytical skills, strategic thinking, and an understanding of market dynamics. By mastering forecasting and financial planning, businesses can navigate uncertainties, allocate resources efficiently, and achieve their strategic goals.

Forecasting involves predicting future financial conditions and performance based on historical data, market trends, and other relevant information. There are several types of forecasting methods, including qualitative and quantitative approaches. Qualitative forecasting relies on expert opinions and market research, making it useful when historical data is limited or when predicting new and emerging trends. Techniques such as the Delphi method, market surveys, and expert panels fall under this category.

Quantitative forecasting, on the other hand, uses mathematical models and statistical techniques to predict future outcomes based on historical data. Time series analysis, regression analysis, and econometric models are common quantitative methods. Time series analysis examines patterns in historical data to forecast future values, while regression analysis explores relationships between variables to predict future trends. Econometric models combine economic theory with statistical methods to forecast economic variables.

Effective forecasting requires selecting the appropriate method based on the context and available data. For instance, a startup with limited historical data might rely more on qualitative methods, while an established company with extensive data might use quantitative techniques. Regardless of the method, the key is to regularly update forecasts as new information becomes available and to continuously refine the models used.

Financial planning involves developing strategies and plans to achieve the financial objectives identified through forecasting. It encompasses budgeting, capital allocation, risk management, and performance monitoring. The financial planning process begins with setting clear financial goals, such as revenue targets, profitability levels, and capital requirements. These goals should be specific, measurable, achievable, relevant, and time-bound (SMART).

Once goals are established, the next step is to create a detailed budget. A budget outlines expected revenues, expenses, and capital expenditures over a specific period, typically a fiscal year. It serves as a financial roadmap, guiding decision-making and resource allocation. Budgets should be realistic yet challenging, encouraging efficiency and cost control while supporting growth initiatives.

Capital allocation is a critical component of financial planning. It involves deciding how to distribute financial resources among various projects, departments, or investments to maximize returns and achieve strategic objectives. Effective capital allocation requires a thorough analysis of potential investments, considering factors such as expected returns, risks, and alignment with strategic goals. Techniques such as net present value (NPV), internal rate of return (IRR), and payback period are commonly used to evaluate investment opportunities.

Risk management is another vital aspect of financial planning. Businesses face various risks, including market volatility, economic downturns, and operational disruptions. Identifying, assessing, and mitigating these risks is essential for maintaining financial stability. Risk management strategies might include diversifying investments, purchasing insurance, and implementing robust internal controls.

Performance monitoring involves regularly reviewing financial performance against the budget and strategic goals. Key performance indicators (KPIs) and financial ratios are used to assess progress and identify areas needing adjustment. Regular financial reports, such as income statements, balance sheets, and cash flow statements, provide valuable insights into a company's financial health and performance. By comparing actual results with forecasts and budgets, businesses can make informed decisions and take corrective actions when necessary.

Consider the story of ABC Manufacturing, a mid-sized company that successfully integrated forecasting and financial planning into its operations. Facing increased competition and market volatility, ABC Manufacturing's management recognized the need for a more structured approach to financial management. They began by enhancing their forecasting capabilities, combining both qualitative and quantitative methods.

The company conducted market surveys and engaged industry experts to gain insights into emerging trends and customer preferences. Simultaneously, they used time series analysis to identify patterns in their historical sales data. By merging these insights, ABC Manufacturing developed more accurate sales forecasts, which formed the basis for their financial planning.

With clear financial goals in place, the company created a detailed budget, aligning resources with strategic priorities. They allocated capital to high-potential projects, such as new product development and market expansion, using NPV and IRR to evaluate potential returns. To manage risks, ABC Manufacturing diversified its product portfolio and established contingency plans for potential market disruptions.

Performance monitoring became an integral part of their financial planning process. Monthly financial reviews allowed management to track progress, identify variances, and adjust strategies promptly. They implemented KPIs such as gross profit margin, return on investment, and inventory turnover to measure efficiency and profitability.

ABC Manufacturing's structured approach to forecasting and financial planning yielded significant benefits. They achieved more accurate sales projections, improved resource allocation, and enhanced financial stability. By continuously refining their processes and adapting to changing market conditions, they maintained a competitive edge and sustained long-term growth.

In summary, forecasting and financial planning are indispensable tools for business success. Forecasting provides a forward-looking perspective, enabling businesses to anticipate future conditions and make informed decisions. Financial planning translates these forecasts into actionable strategies, guiding resource allocation, risk management, and performance monitoring. By integrating these practices into their operations, businesses can navigate uncertainties and drive sustainable growth.

Decision-making is a critical skill for business leaders and managers at all levels. Utilizing the right tools and techniques can transform how decisions are made, leading to more effective outcomes and successful strategies. Imagine you're leading a mid-sized manufacturing company and face the challenge of deciding whether to invest in new machinery or expand the current workforce. The decision isn't straightforward, but with the right tools and techniques, you can navigate this complexity with confidence.

One of the foundational tools for decision-making is the SWOT analysis. This tool helps you evaluate your company's internal Strengths and Weaknesses, as well as external Opportunities and Threats. Conducting a SWOT analysis provides a comprehensive view of your business environment. For instance, if your manufacturing company excels in innovation (a strength) but struggles with high production costs (a weakness), and you see a market trend towards automation (an opportunity), while facing increasing competition (a threat), you can weigh these factors to make a more informed decision.

Another powerful technique is the Decision Matrix, also known as the Pugh Matrix or Multi-Criteria Decision Analysis (MCDA). This tool helps prioritize and evaluate different options based on specific criteria. Imagine you have three potential investments: new machinery, workforce expansion, and a marketing campaign. By listing these options and scoring them against criteria such as cost, potential return on investment, implementation time, and risk, you can objectively compare and prioritize them. The Decision Matrix not only provides a clear visual representation of your options but also ensures that your decision is based on a balanced consideration of all relevant factors.

Cost-Benefit Analysis (CBA) is another indispensable tool. This technique involves comparing the costs and benefits of different options to determine which one offers the greatest net benefit. For example, when deciding whether to invest in new machinery, you would calculate the total costs (purchase price, installation, maintenance) and weigh them against the anticipated benefits (increased production efficiency, reduced labor costs, higher quality output). The option with the highest net benefit—benefits minus costs—would be the most viable choice. CBA is particularly useful for financial decisions, providing a clear economic rationale for your choices.

Scenario Analysis is a technique that involves creating multiple scenarios to predict and evaluate the impact of different decisions under various conditions. This is particularly useful in uncertain environments. For example, if your company is considering entering a new market, you could develop scenarios based on different market conditions (e.g., high demand, moderate demand, low demand) and assess how each scenario affects your business. Scenario Analysis helps in understanding potential risks and opportunities, allowing you to prepare contingency plans and make more resilient decisions.

The Delphi Technique is a structured communication method used for making decisions in complex situations. It involves a panel of experts who anonymously provide their opinions and feedback over multiple rounds. After each round, a facilitator summarizes the responses and shares them with the panel, allowing participants to revise their views based on the feedback. This iterative process continues until a consensus is reached. The Delphi Technique is particularly effective for strategic decisions that require expert judgment and consensus, such as launching a new product line or entering a new market.

Decision Trees are another valuable tool, especially for decisions involving multiple stages or complex scenarios. A decision tree is a graphical representation of possible outcomes, where each branch represents a different decision path and its potential consequences. For instance, if your company is considering launching a new product, a decision tree can help map out the different stages—from development to marketing to sales—and the associated risks and rewards at each stage. This visual aid helps clarify the decision-making process, making it easier to evaluate the long-term implications of each choice.

In addition to these tools, incorporating data analytics into your decision-making process can significantly enhance the accuracy and effectiveness of your decisions. Data analytics involves using statistical and computational techniques to analyze large datasets and extract meaningful insights. For example, by analyzing sales data, customer feedback, and market trends, you can identify patterns and correlations that inform your decisions. Predictive analytics, which uses historical data to forecast future trends, can be particularly useful for making proactive decisions and staying ahead of the competition.

Mind Mapping is a creative technique that helps visualize the relationship between different aspects of a decision. It involves creating a diagram where a central idea is connected to related ideas, forming a network of concepts. This technique is particularly useful for brainstorming and exploring complex problems. For example, when planning a new marketing strategy, a mind map can help organize your thoughts, identify key elements (target audience, channels, messaging), and explore their interconnections. By visually mapping out your ideas, you can uncover new insights and connections that might not be apparent through linear thinking.

The Pareto Analysis, also known as the 80/20 rule, is a technique that helps prioritize decisions based on their impact. According to the Pareto principle, 80% of the results come from 20% of the causes. By identifying and focusing on the vital few factors that have the most significant impact, you can allocate your resources more effectively. For example, if you find that 80% of your sales come from 20% of your products, you can concentrate your marketing efforts and resources on those key products to maximize your returns. Pareto Analysis helps you identify where to focus your efforts for the greatest impact, making it an invaluable tool for efficient resource allocation.

Chapter 5: Ensuring Accuracy and Compliance

Internal Controls and Fraud Prevention

Fraud is a pervasive threat in today's business environment, affecting organizations of all sizes and industries. Establishing robust internal controls is crucial to mitigating this risk and ensuring operational integrity. Imagine a small retail company that recently discovered a significant inventory discrepancy. Investigating further, they found that an employee had been siphoning off merchandise for months. This scenario underscores the importance of internal controls and fraud prevention measures in safeguarding company assets and maintaining trust.

Internal controls are processes and procedures implemented to ensure the reliability of financial reporting, compliance with laws and regulations, and the efficiency of operations. These controls serve as the first line of defense against fraud, errors, and inefficiencies. One fundamental aspect of internal controls is the segregation of duties. This principle involves dividing responsibilities among different employees to reduce the risk of errors and prevent fraudulent activities. For example, in the accounts payable process, one employee should authorize payments, another should process the payments, and a third should reconcile the bank statements. This separation of duties ensures that no single individual has control over all aspects of a financial transaction, making it more difficult for fraudulent activities to go undetected.

Reconciliation is another critical internal control measure. Regular reconciliation of accounts helps identify discrepancies between the company's records and external statements, such as bank or vendor statements. For instance, reconciling the accounts receivable ledger with customer payment records ensures that all payments are accurately recorded and any discrepancies are promptly addressed. This process helps detect and prevent errors and fraudulent activities, providing assurance that the financial records are accurate and complete.

Physical controls are essential in preventing unauthorized access to assets and sensitive information. For example, a manufacturing company should have secure storage areas for raw materials and finished goods, with access restricted to authorized personnel only. Similarly, sensitive information, such as financial records and customer data, should be protected through secure access controls and encryption. Implementing physical controls helps safeguard assets and data, reducing the risk of theft, loss, or unauthorized use.

Monitoring and auditing are pivotal in maintaining the effectiveness of internal controls. Regular internal and external audits provide an independent assessment of the company's internal control environment, identifying weaknesses and recommending improvements. For example, an internal audit might reveal that the company's expense reimbursement process lacks adequate oversight, leading to potential misuse of funds. By addressing these findings, the company can strengthen its internal controls and reduce the risk of fraud.

Fraud prevention also relies heavily on creating a culture of integrity and ethical behavior within the organization. Establishing a strong ethical framework begins with the tone at the top. Leadership must demonstrate a commitment to ethical conduct and set clear expectations for behavior throughout the organization. For example, a company's code of conduct should outline acceptable behavior and provide guidelines for handling ethical dilemmas. Regular training sessions on ethics and fraud awareness can reinforce these principles and ensure that employees understand their role in preventing fraud.

Whistleblower programs are an effective tool for fraud prevention. These programs encourage employees to report suspicious activities without fear of retaliation. For instance, an anonymous hotline or secure online reporting system can provide a safe channel for employees to report concerns. By fostering an environment where employees feel comfortable reporting unethical behavior, companies can detect and address potential fraud early, before it escalates into a more significant issue.

Technology plays a crucial role in enhancing internal controls and fraud prevention measures. Automated systems can streamline processes, reduce manual errors, and provide real-time monitoring and reporting. For example, implementing an enterprise resource planning (ERP) system can integrate various business functions, such as accounting, inventory management, and procurement, providing a comprehensive view of the company's operations. Automated alerts can notify management of unusual transactions or deviations from established procedures, enabling timely intervention.

Data analytics is another powerful tool in the fight against fraud. By analyzing large datasets, companies can identify patterns and anomalies that may indicate fraudulent activities. For instance, a retail company might use data analytics to detect unusual purchasing patterns or identify employees with unusually high voided transactions. By leveraging data analytics, companies can proactively monitor for potential fraud and implement targeted controls to mitigate risks.

Cybersecurity measures are also critical in preventing fraud, particularly in today's digital age. Protecting against cyber threats requires a multi-layered approach, including firewalls, intrusion detection systems, and regular security assessments. For example, a company should implement strong password policies, multi-factor authentication, and regular software updates to protect against unauthorized access. Employee training on cybersecurity best practices, such as recognizing phishing emails and avoiding suspicious links, is also essential in reducing the risk of cyber fraud.

Continuous improvement is key to maintaining effective internal controls and fraud prevention measures. Companies should regularly review and update their internal controls to adapt to changing business environments and emerging threats. For example, as a company expands into new markets or adopts new technologies, its internal controls should be reassessed to ensure they remain effective. Regular feedback from employees and stakeholders can provide valuable insights into potential weaknesses and areas for improvement.

Case studies of successful fraud prevention can provide valuable lessons and insights. Consider the case of a financial services company that implemented a comprehensive fraud prevention program, including enhanced internal controls, regular audits, and a robust whistle blower program. This company also integrated advanced data analytics to monitor transaction patterns and detect anomalies in real-time. By fostering a culture of transparency and accountability, the organization significantly reduced incidents of fraud and improved overall operational efficiency. The success of this program highlights the importance of a multi-faceted approach to fraud prevention, combining technological solutions with strong ethical practices and continuous monitoring.

Auditing, both internal and external, plays a crucial role in the governance and financial integrity of organizations. These audits provide assurance that a company's financial statements are accurate, operations are efficient, and compliance with regulations is maintained. Understanding the differences between internal and external audits, their respective methodologies, and their significance is essential for any business aiming to uphold high standards of accountability and transparency.

Internal auditing is conducted by employees within the organization. The primary objective here is to improve internal processes and ensure that the company's operations are running efficiently. Internal auditors assess the effectiveness of risk management, control, and governance processes. They work closely with management to identify weaknesses and recommend improvements. This proactive approach helps in preventing issues before they escalate into significant problems.

Consider the case of a mid-sized retail company, RetailMart, which decided to strengthen its internal audit function. The company was growing rapidly, and with expansion came complexities in operations. The internal audit team at RetailMart started by mapping out all critical processes, from supply chain management to sales operations. They identified key risk areas, such as inventory management and financial reporting, where errors or fraud could occur.

The audit team then developed a comprehensive audit plan. They conducted detailed reviews of inventory records, cross-checking them against physical stock levels to ensure accuracy. They also assessed the effectiveness of the company's internal controls by testing transaction approvals and authorization processes. Through these audits, RetailMart discovered several discrepancies in inventory records and instances where controls were bypassed.

By addressing these issues, RetailMart not only improved its operational efficiency but also reduced the risk of financial misstatements. The internal audit team's recommendations led to the implementation of a more robust inventory management system and stricter control procedures. This proactive approach to internal auditing helped the company maintain its growth trajectory without compromising on operational integrity.

External auditing, on the other hand, is performed by independent firms outside the organization. The primary goal of an external audit is to provide an objective evaluation of the company's financial statements. External auditors ensure that the financial reports are free from material misstatements and comply with accounting standards and regulations. This type of audit provides assurance to stakeholders, such as investors, regulators, and creditors, about the accuracy and reliability of the financial information presented by the company.

Take, for instance, the experience of Tech Innovations Inc., a technology firm preparing to go public. To ensure that its financial statements were accurate and ready for scrutiny by potential investors, Tech Innovations hired an external audit firm. The external auditors performed a thorough examination of the company's financial records, including balance sheets, income statements, and cash flow statements.

The auditors tested the validity of transactions, verified account balances, and assessed the overall financial reporting process. They also evaluated the company's compliance with relevant accounting standards and regulations. During the audit, the external auditors identified several areas where Tech Innovations needed to improve its financial reporting practices, such as more accurate revenue recognition and better documentation of expenses.

The insights provided by the external auditors were invaluable for Tech Innovations. The company made the necessary adjustments to its financial statements, ensuring they were accurate and compliant. This rigorous external audit process not only prepared Tech Innovations for its public offering but also boosted investor confidence in the company's financial integrity.

Both internal and external audits follow systematic methodologies to achieve their objectives. Internal audits typically involve a continuous and iterative process, where the audit team plans, executes, and monitors audits throughout the year. They begin with a risk assessment to identify areas that require attention. Based on this assessment, the audit team develops an audit plan, detailing the scope, objectives, and timelines for each audit engagement.

During the execution phase, internal auditors gather evidence through various techniques, such as interviews, document reviews, and data analysis. They then analyze the findings, identify control weaknesses, and make recommendations for improvement. The final step involves reporting the audit results to management and the board of directors, followed by monitoring the implementation of recommended actions.

External audits, in contrast, are typically conducted annually and follow a more structured process. The external audit begins with an engagement letter, outlining the scope and objectives of the audit. The auditors then perform a preliminary assessment to understand the company's business operations, internal controls, and risk environment. This understanding helps them design an audit plan tailored to the specific needs of the company.

The next phase involves detailed testing of account balances and transactions. External auditors use sampling techniques to select a representative subset of transactions for testing. They verify the accuracy and completeness of these transactions by examining supporting documentation, such as invoices, receipts, and contracts. The auditors also assess the effectiveness of the company's internal controls by performing walkthroughs and control tests.

Once the testing is complete, the auditors analyze the results and prepare an audit report. This report includes their opinion on whether the financial statements present a true and fair view of the company's financial position. If material misstatements are identified, the auditors discuss these findings with management and recommend adjustments. The final audit report is then presented to the company's stakeholders, providing them with assurance about the reliability of the financial information.

Both internal and external audits are essential for ensuring the robustness of a company's financial reporting and operational processes. While they serve different purposes and audiences, their interplay contributes to a comprehensive framework of checks and balances within the organization.

Compliance with Accounting Standards: GAAP and IFRS

Navigating the landscape of accounting standards is crucial for businesses to ensure transparency, consistency, and comparability in their financial reporting. Two primary frameworks dominate the global accounting stage: Generally Accepted Accounting Principles (GAAP) and International Financial Reporting Standards (IFRS). Understanding their nuances, applications, and implications is essential for companies operating in domestic and international markets.

GAAP, predominantly used in the United States, is a comprehensive set of rules and guidelines established by the Financial Accounting Standards Board (FASB). It is designed to ensure that financial statements are consistent, reliable, and comparable across different entities. GAAP encompasses a wide range of principles, including revenue recognition, expense matching, and full disclosure. These principles provide a structured approach to financial reporting, which helps stakeholders make informed decisions based on accurate and standardized financial information.

Consider the case of an American manufacturing company, AutoTech Inc., which adheres to GAAP in its financial reporting. AutoTech follows GAAP's revenue recognition principle, which mandates that revenue should only be recognized when it is earned and realizable. This means AutoTech records revenue only when it has delivered the product to the customer and the payment is reasonably assured. By adhering to this principle, AutoTech ensures that its financial statements accurately reflect its financial position and performance, preventing the premature recognition of revenue and potential financial misstatements.

GAAP also emphasizes the matching principle, which requires that expenses be matched with the revenues they help generate. For AutoTech, this means recording the cost of goods sold at the same time as the related revenue. This principle ensures that the company's income statement accurately portrays its profitability, providing a clear picture of how operational costs impact revenue generation. By following GAAP, AutoTech not only complies with regulatory standards but also enhances the credibility of its financial reports.

In contrast, IFRS is a global accounting framework developed by the International Accounting Standards Board (IASB). It is widely adopted outside the United States, providing a common accounting language that enhances comparability across international boundaries. IFRS focuses on principles rather than detailed rules, offering a more flexible approach to financial reporting. This flexibility allows companies to better reflect the economic substance of transactions, which can vary significantly across different industries and regions.

Imagine a multinational corporation, GlobalTech Ltd., headquartered in the United Kingdom and operating in multiple countries. GlobalTech adopts IFRS for its consolidated financial statements to ensure consistency and comparability across its diverse operations. One of the key principles of IFRS is the recognition of revenue based on the transfer of control rather than the strict criteria outlined in GAAP. For instance, GlobalTech recognizes revenue when it transfers control of a product or service to the customer, which may occur at different points depending on the contract terms and delivery conditions. This approach allows GlobalTech to align its revenue recognition with the actual economic events, providing a more accurate depiction of its financial performance.

IFRS also emphasizes the concept of fair value measurement, which requires assets and liabilities to be measured at their current market value. This principle is particularly relevant for GlobalTech, which holds a significant portfolio of financial instruments. By measuring these instruments at fair value, GlobalTech provides stakeholders with a more accurate and timely view of its financial position, reflecting the current market conditions. This approach enhances the relevance of the financial statements, enabling investors and other stakeholders to make better-informed decisions.

The adoption of IFRS can also have significant implications for companies transitioning from GAAP. For example, a U.S.-based company planning to expand its operations globally might consider adopting IFRS to align with international reporting standards. This transition requires a thorough understanding of the differences between GAAP and IFRS, as well as comprehensive planning and implementation. The company must assess the impact of IFRS on its financial statements, internal controls, and business processes.

One major difference between GAAP and IFRS lies in their treatment of inventory. Under GAAP, companies can use the Last-In, First-Out (LIFO) method to value their inventory, which can result in lower taxable income during periods of inflation. However, IFRS prohibits the use of LIFO, requiring companies to use either the First-In, First-Out (FIFO) method or the weighted-average cost method. For a U.S. company transitioning to IFRS, this change could lead to higher reported inventory values and potentially higher taxable income, necessitating adjustments to financial strategies and tax planning.

Another significant difference is the treatment of leases. GAAP and IFRS both require companies to recognize most leases on the balance sheet, but there are differences in the classification and measurement of lease liabilities and right-of-use assets. Under IFRS, there is a single lessee accounting model that requires all leases to be classified as finance leases, whereas GAAP differentiates between operating and finance leases. Transitioning to IFRS may require companies to reevaluate their lease agreements and make necessary adjustments to their financial statements.

Despite these differences, the goal of both GAAP and IFRS is to provide high-quality, transparent, and comparable financial information. Companies must carefully evaluate which framework best suits their needs based on their operational scope, regulatory environment, and stakeholder requirements. For businesses primarily operating in the United States, GAAP remains the standard due to regulatory mandates and market expectations. Conversely, multinational corporations and entities aiming for global investment often lean towards IFRS to streamline their financial reporting across various jurisdictions.

Ethical Considerations in Accounting

Ethical considerations in accounting are vital to maintaining the integrity, transparency, and trustworthiness of financial reporting. Accountants, as stewards of financial information, play a crucial role in ensuring that the data presented to stakeholders is accurate and reliable. Ethical lapses in accounting can lead to disastrous consequences, including financial losses, legal penalties, and a loss of public trust. Therefore, understanding and adhering to ethical principles is fundamental for both individual accountants and the organizations they serve.

Consider the story of Enron, one of the most infamous cases of accounting fraud in history. Enron executives, in collusion with its accounting firm, Arthur Andersen, engaged in widespread accounting fraud to hide the company's financial losses and inflate its stock price. They used complex financial structures and off-balance-sheet entities to mislead investors and regulators. When the fraud was eventually uncovered, Enron declared bankruptcy, thousands of employees lost their jobs and savings, and Arthur Andersen, one of the largest accounting firms in the world, was dissolved. The Enron scandal underscored the catastrophic impact of unethical accounting practices and led to significant regulatory reforms, including the Sarbanes-Oxley Act of 2002.

At the core of ethical accounting is the adherence to a code of conduct that emphasizes integrity, objectivity, professional competence, confidentiality, and professional behavior. Integrity involves being straightforward and honest in all professional and business relationships. This means avoiding any actions or omissions that could discredit the profession. For instance, accountants must not engage in activities that could lead to conflicts of interest or compromise their ability to remain impartial.

Objectivity requires accountants to be impartial, unbiased, and free from conflicts of interest. This principle is critical when making judgments or providing opinions that could affect the financial decisions of others. For example, an accountant must not allow personal relationships or financial interests to influence their professional judgment. They should always strive to present financial information fairly and without bias.

Professional competence and due care mandate that accountants maintain their knowledge and skills at a level required to ensure that clients or employers receive competent professional services. This involves a commitment to continuous learning and staying updated with the latest developments in accounting standards, regulations, and best practices. An accountant who fails to keep their skills current may inadvertently provide incorrect advice or services, potentially leading to financial harm for their clients or employers.

Confidentiality is another cornerstone of ethical accounting. Accountants often have access to sensitive financial information, and it is their duty to protect this information from unauthorized disclosure. This means not only safeguarding physical and digital records but also being mindful of how and where they discuss confidential matters. Breaches of confidentiality can damage a client's or employer's competitive position and erode trust in the accounting profession.

Professional behavior requires accountants to comply with relevant laws and regulations and avoid any conduct that discredits the profession. This includes adhering to ethical guidelines set by professional accounting bodies, such as the American Institute of Certified Public Accountants (AICPA) in the United States or the International Federation of Accountants (IFAC) globally. Accountants must also be vigilant against unethical behavior by others, including reporting any suspicious activities or breaches of ethical standards.

One practical aspect of maintaining ethical standards in accounting is the implementation of robust internal controls and corporate governance mechanisms. Internal controls are processes and procedures put in place by an organization to ensure the integrity of financial and accounting information, promote accountability, and prevent fraud. Effective internal controls include segregation of duties, regular audits, and clear policies and procedures for financial transactions.

Corporate governance, on the other hand, involves the system of rules, practices, and processes by which a company is directed and controlled. Good corporate governance ensures that an organization's leadership acts in the best interests of its stakeholders, including shareholders, employees, customers, and the community. This includes establishing an independent board of directors, promoting transparency, and ensuring accountability.

Consider the case of a mid-sized manufacturing company, GreenTech Industries, which implemented a comprehensive ethics program to reinforce ethical behavior among its accounting staff. This program included regular ethics training, a confidential whistleblower hotline, and strict enforcement of internal controls. The company also established an ethics committee responsible for overseeing ethical issues and ensuring compliance with its code of conduct.

Through these measures, GreenTech Industries was able to cultivate a culture of integrity and accountability. Employees felt empowered to report unethical behavior without fear of retaliation, and the company's leadership demonstrated a strong commitment to ethical principles. As a result, GreenTech Industries not only avoided major ethical breaches but also enhanced its reputation as a trustworthy and responsible business.

Another important aspect of ethical accounting is the role of professional accounting bodies in setting and enforcing ethical standards. These organizations provide guidance, resources, and support to help accountants navigate ethical dilemmas and maintain high standards of professional conduct. They also play a crucial role in disciplining members who violate ethical guidelines, thereby upholding the integrity of the profession.

Leveraging Technology for Accuracy and Compliance

In the modern landscape of accounting, leveraging technology for accuracy and compliance has become indispensable. The evolution of digital tools and software has transformed how accountants perform their duties, ensuring more precise financial reporting and adherence to regulatory standards. Embracing these technological advancements not only enhances efficiency but also mitigates the risks associated with human error and fraud.

Consider the story of a small accounting firm, Smith & Co., which embraced cloud-based accounting software to streamline its operations. Previously, the firm relied on manual processes and spreadsheets, which were time-consuming and prone to errors. By transitioning to a cloud-based solution, Smith & Co. significantly reduced the time spent on data entry and reconciliation. The software's automated features, such as real-time data updates and integration with banking systems, ensured that financial information was always current and accurate. Consequently, the firm could provide more timely and reliable services to its clients, enhancing its reputation and client satisfaction.

One of the primary benefits of leveraging technology in accounting is the automation of routine tasks. Automation tools can handle repetitive activities such as data entry, invoice processing, and payroll management. By automating these tasks, accountants can focus on more strategic activities like financial analysis and advisory services. Automation not only saves time but also reduces the likelihood of errors that can occur with manual processes. For instance, automated bank reconciliation tools can match transactions with bank statements, flag discrepancies, and ensure that financial records are accurate and complete.

In addition to automation, advanced accounting software offers robust features for compliance management. These tools are designed to help organizations adhere to various regulatory requirements, such as the Sarbanes-Oxley Act, Generally Accepted Accounting Principles (GAAP), and International Financial Reporting Standards (IFRS). Compliance features often include audit trails, which provide a detailed log of all transactions and changes made within the system. This transparency is crucial during audits, as it allows auditors to trace the origins and alterations of financial data, ensuring that all transactions are legitimate and properly documented.

Moreover, technology facilitates real-time financial reporting and analysis. Traditional accounting methods often involve a lag between the occurrence of financial events and their recording and analysis. With real-time reporting tools, businesses can access up-to-date financial information at any time. This immediacy allows for better decision-making and quicker responses to financial issues. For example, a company using real-time financial dashboards can monitor key performance indicators (KPIs) and financial ratios continuously. If any metric deviates from the expected range, management can investigate and address the issue promptly, preventing potential financial problems.

Data security is another critical aspect of leveraging technology in accounting. As accountants handle sensitive financial information, ensuring its protection is paramount. Modern accounting software incorporates advanced security measures such as encryption, multi-factor authentication, and regular security updates. These features protect against unauthorized access and cyber threats, safeguarding the integrity and confidentiality of financial data. Additionally, cloud-based solutions often provide secure backup and disaster recovery options, ensuring that data is not lost or compromised in case of hardware failures or other emergencies.

Consider the case of a mid-sized retail company, Retail Dynamics, which faced a significant data breach due to inadequate security measures in its legacy accounting system. Customer and financial data were exposed, leading to financial losses and reputational damage. To prevent future incidents,

Retail Dynamics adopted a cloud-based accounting solution with robust security features. The new system encrypted all sensitive data and required multi-factor authentication for access. Regular security audits and updates further ensured that the company's data remained protected against evolving cyber threats.

Furthermore, leveraging technology enhances collaboration and accessibility in accounting. Cloud-based accounting platforms enable multiple users to access and work on financial data simultaneously from different locations. This capability is particularly beneficial for organizations with distributed teams or remote work arrangements. Collaborative tools such as shared workspaces and real-time document editing facilitate seamless communication and coordination among team members. For example, a multinational corporation can have its finance team in New York collaborate with its accounting department in London, ensuring that financial reporting and compliance efforts are unified and efficient.

Another significant advantage of using technology in accounting is the ability to harness big data and analytics. Advanced analytics tools can process vast amounts of financial data to uncover insights and trends that would be difficult to detect manually. Predictive analytics, for instance, can forecast future financial performance based on historical data, helping businesses plan and strategize more effectively. Descriptive analytics can provide detailed reports on past performance, identifying areas for improvement and guiding decision-making. By leveraging these analytical capabilities, accountants can offer more valuable insights and recommendations to their clients or organizations.

Consider a scenario where a manufacturing company, TechManufacture, implemented an advanced analytics tool to analyze its financial data. The tool helped the company identify patterns in its cash flow, revealing that certain customers consistently paid late, impacting its liquidity. With this insight, TechManufacture implemented stricter credit policies and improved its cash flow management, ultimately enhancing its financial stability. The ability to analyze and act on financial data in this manner demonstrates the transformative potential of technology in accounting.

Lastly, the integration of artificial intelligence (AI) and machine learning (ML) into accounting software is revolutionizing the field. AI algorithms can process and analyze vast amounts of data more quickly and accurately than humans. Machine learning models can learn from historical data to identify patterns, detect anomalies, and predict future trends. For example, AI-powered expense management tools can automatically categorize expenses, flag unusual transactions, and provide insights into spending patterns. These capabilities reduce the workload on accountants and enhance the accuracy of financial reporting.